The media's watching Va[ult].
Here's a sampling of our coverage.

> the most trusted name in career information™

VAULT CAREER GUIDE TO
HEDGE FUNDS

VAULT CAREER GUIDE TO
HEDGE FUNDS

**ADITI A. DAVARE, HOLLY GOODRICH,
MICHAEL MARTINEZ
AND THE STAFF OF VAULT**

4/25/08

Library of Congress CIP Data is available.

ISBN 10: 1-58131-534-1

ISBN 13: 978-1-58131-534-9

Printed in the United States of America

ACKNOWLEDGMENTS

Vault's acknowledgments: Thanks to everyone who had a hand in making this book possible. We are also extremely grateful to Vault's entire staff for all their help in the editorial, production and marketing processes. Vault also would like to acknowledge the support of our investors, clients, employees, family, and friends. Thank you!

Table of Contents

Visit the Vault Finance Career Channel at **www.vault.com/finance** — with
insider firm profiles, message boards, the Vault Finance Job Board and more.

VAULT CAREER LIBRARY   **xiii**

Visit the Vault Finance Career Channel at **www.vault.com/finance** — with
insider firm profiles, message boards, the Vault Finance Job Board and more.

VAULT CAREER LIBRARY   **xv**

Introduction

What is a Hedge Fund?

A recent survey by *Absolute Return* magazine showed that U.S hedge funds now control some $1.2 billion in assets as of Jan. 1, 2007. Globally, assets under management is as high as $2 trillion. Hedge funds have grown to the point where they are considered one of the biggest players in nearly every market—stocks, bonds, commodities and derivatives.

Hedge funds are considered an "alternative investment" vehicle. The term "alternative investment" is the general term under which unregulated funds operate; this includes private equity and real estate funds. The total "alternative" category (which would include private equity and real estate) is not covered within the scope of this book but it is useful to know that often people refer to hedge funds as an alternative investment. Mainstream funds are investment funds that everyday investors can purchase; mutual funds are the prime example of a mainstream fund.

Since the early 1990s, hedge funds have grown tremendously, not only in terms of assets under management, but also in the amount of media attention they've garnered for their brash strategies and the massive returns many have generated. Although they may remain a mystery to the general public, their effect on the global marketplace is felt more strongly with each passing day. Hedge fund managers are constantly trying to find new ways to take advantage of the market's inefficiencies in order to generate "absolute returns"—posting returns in the black each year, no matter what the overall market does. During the bull market that started in late 2002, that's been pretty simple—when stocks around the world are surging, it's relatively easy to make money. But in the coming years, hedge funds will be sorely tested as the markets settle down after a four-year run and absolute returns are more difficult to come by.

In this chapter, we will explore what it means to be a hedge fund in these changing times, as fund managers try not only to continue generating outsized returns, but also go back to the core purpose of hedge funds—to hedge against risk.

Visit the Vault Finance Career Channel at **www.vault.com/finance** — with insider firm profiles, message boards, the Vault Finance Job Board and more.

VAULT CAREER LIBRARY

1

So what exactly is a hedge fund? The term "hedge fund" is an industry term and the following is one way to define it:

A Concise Definition of "Hedge Fund"

Definition: A private, unregistered investment pool encompassing all types of investment funds, companies and private partnerships that can use a variety of investment techniques such as borrowing money through leverage, selling short, derivatives for directional investing and options.

During the early years of the hedge fund industry (1950s—1970s), the term "hedge fund" was used to describe the "hedging" strategy used by managers at the time. "Hedging" refers to the hedge fund manager making additional trades in an attempt to counterbalance any risk involved with the existing positions in the portfolio. Hedging can be accomplished in many different ways but the most basic technique is to purchase a long position and a secondary short position in a similar security (see the Gap stores example on page 9). This is used to offset price fluctuations and is an effective way of neutralizing the effects of market conditions.

Today, the term "hedge fund" tells an investor nothing about the underlying investment activities, similar to the term "mutual fund." So how do you figure out what the hedge fund manager does? You are able to figure out a little more about the underlying investment activities by understanding the trading/investment strategies that the hedge fund manager states he trades. The "investment strategy" is the investment approach or the techniques used by the hedge fund manager to have positive returns on the investments. If a manager says he trades long/short equity then you know he is buying undervalued equities and selling overvalued equities. Although this description is the long/short equity strategy at its most basic, it is important to understand the strategies that the manager says he employs. More details follow in the strategy section.

So now you have a better idea of what the definition of a hedge fund is. To know more about the industry, you will need to appreciate basic finance and how it operates. This book is not going to cover the very basics of finance; it is assumed that the reader has some knowledge of what stocks, bonds and commodities are and the way these markets work. In order to ensure that you fully appreciate the specific language used when discussing the hedge fund industry, we have highlighted some of the very key points you will need to know.

Newspaper and industry magazines tend to have a language of their own when discussing the hedge fund industry, its managers and strategies. It is important that you recognize a few basic terms. It is also useful to really understand these concepts for a job interview. Here are the basics. (A more detailed glossary is at the back of the book.)

Basic Hedge Fund Terminology

Alternative investing

Hedge funds fall under the category of alternative investments and may be referred to as such. The "alternative investing" category encompasses other private investments such as private equity and real estate. Mainstream investing refers mainly to mutual funds or other investments that everyone can invest in (without needing a certain net worth to do so).

Arbitrage

Arbitrage involves the simultaneous purchase and sale of a security or pair of similar securities to profit from a pricing discrepancy. This could be the purchase and sale of the identical item in different markets to make profits— for example there could be an arbitrage opportunity in the price of gold that is sold more expensively in London than in New York. In this case, the arbitrageur would buy gold in New York and sell in London, profiting from the price differential. This could be applied to a variety of transactions: foreign exchange, mortgages, futures, stocks, bonds, silver or other commodities in one market for sale in another at a profit.

Asset classes

Asset class means a type of investment, such as stocks, bonds, real estate, or cash. For example: stocks are a separate asset class from bonds.

Visit the Vault Finance Career Channel at **www.vault.com/finance** — with insider firm profiles, message boards, the Vault Finance Job Board and more.

VAULT CAREER LIBRARY

3

Convertible bond

Convertible bond is a bond that can be exchanged, at the option of the holder, for a specific number of shares of a company's stock (preferred or common). Convertible bonds tend to have lower interest rates than the non-convertibles because they also increase in value as the price of the underlying stock rises. In this way, convertible bonds offer some of the benefits of both stock and bonds since they earn interest like bonds and appreciate in value like stocks.

Credit trading

Credit trading involves the buying and selling of packaged, securitized debt. For example, mortgage lenders will bundle and sell their mortgage credits as a security, which a hedge fund might buy as part of an expected steady stream of income. The lender gets the benefit of its mortgage money up front, while the hedge fund benefits from the longer-term flow of payments.

Currency

Currency trading and swaps have proven to be a lucrative form of trading for hedge funds in the increasingly global marketplace. Not only can currencies themselves be traded—buying up yen at a low rate, then exchanging at a better rate—but hedge funds can also buy and sell securities in different currencies. A hedge fund might buy up a promising stock trading in Japan by changing dollars to yen, then buying the stock. Once the fund sells, it not only profits from an increased stock price, but also from a better exchange rate, if it plays the trade correctly.

Derivative

A financial instrument whose characteristics and value depend upon the characteristics and value of an underlier, typically a commodity, bond, equity or currency. Examples of derivatives include futures and options. Hedge fund managers purchase or sell derivatives to manage the risk associated with the underlying security, to protect against fluctuations in value, or to profit from periods of inactivity or decline.

Equity (stock)

Ownership interest in a corporation in the form of common stock or preferred stock.

Fixed income (bond)

A fixed income security is a bond, a debt investment that provides a return in the form of fixed periodic payments (coupons) and eventual return of principle at maturity. Types of bonds include corporate bonds, municipal bonds, treasury bonds, treasury notes and treasury bills. Detailed descriptions of these bonds are located in the glossary in the back of the book.

Hedge fund

A "private, unregistered investment pool" encompassing all types of investment funds, companies and private partnerships that can use a variety of investment techniques such as borrowing money through leverage, selling short, derivatives for directional investing and options.

Leverage

Leverage measures the amount of assets being funded by each investment dollar. The primary source of leverage is from borrowing from financial institutions; an example in everyday terms is a house mortgage. Leverage is essentially borrowing by hedge funds using their assets in the fund as a pledge of collateral toward the loan. The hedge fund manager then uses the loan to buy more securities. (The amount of leverage typically used by the fund is shown as a percentage of the fund.) For example, if the fund has $1,000,000 and is borrowing another $2,000,000, to bring the total dollars invested to $3,000,000, then the leverage used is 200 percent.

Limited partnership

The hedge fund is organized with a general partner, who manages the business and assumes legal debts and obligations, and one or more limited partners, who are liable only to the extent of their investments. Limited partners also enjoy rights to the partnership's cash flow, but are not liable for company obligations.

Visit the Vault Finance Career Channel at **www.vault.com/finance** — with
insider firm profiles, message boards, the Vault Finance Job Board and more.

VAULT CAREER LIBRARY

5

Long

Whenever you purchase a security or bond, in the industry this is known as going "long." This means that you have bought the security or bond.

Money manager (hedge fund manager)

A portfolio/investment manager, the person ultimately responsible for a securities portfolio.

Options

A "put" option gives the holder the right to sell the underlying stock at a specified price (strike price) on or before a given date (exercise date).

A "call" option gives the holder the right to buy the underlying stock at specified price (strike price) on or before a given date (exercise date).

The seller of these options is referred to as the "writer"—many hedge funds will often write options in accordance with their strategies. Most advanced traders can be writers of options. Many people who invest on behalf of themselves are able to trade (and thus write) options in their own brokerage account. The brokerage firm will likely ensure that the person has enough knowledge about the risks involved with buying and selling (writing) options.

Prime brokerage

Prime brokers offer hedge fund clients various tools and services such as securities lending, trading platforms, cash management, risk management and settlements for administration of the hedge fund. The prime brokerage department is located within a larger investment bank.

Private equity and leveraged buyouts

Over the past three years or so, hedge funds have become increasingly active in taking public companies private. Since the Sarbanes-Oxley corporate governance law was passed in 2002, some public companies have been burdened, if not overwhelmed, with the new reporting practices these regulations have engendered. Instead of having to appease both the Securities and Exchange Commission and shareholders expecting consistent earnings growth, some companies have opted to go private in order to make the kind of difficult choices and long-term investments needed to thrive. Along with private equity firms, which are dedicated to buying and turning public companies around, hedge funds have contributed billions to taking companies private. These companies are generally then free to make capital investments without provoking the ire of Wall Street, and then are either sold to another company or taken public again in an initial public offering—at which point the hedge funds and private equity firms see the returns on their investment. While considered a long-term investment, some hedge funds and private equity firms have seen immediate returns by leveraging the companies—issuing corporate bonds—in order to give investors a more immediate pay-off before the private company is either sold to a larger enterprise or taken public once again.

Real estate investments

The surging housing market of the first half of this decade saw a number of hedge funds getting into the game in a variety of ways, from buying up commodity futures used in home construction to purchasing land and even buildings. Indeed, some hedge funds have arms that act as real estate investment trusts, making money on the leases paid on various residential and commercial properties. The downturn in the housing market, which started in late 2005, did not have a major effect on commercial real estate, and some hedge funds continue to make money by buying and leasing everything from industrial parks to major skyscrapers.

Short selling

Short selling involves the selling of a security that the seller does not own. Short sellers believe that the stock price will fall (as opposed to buying long, when one believes the price will rise) and that they will be able to repurchase the stock at a lower price in the future. Thus, they will profit from selling the stock at a higher price then repurchase it in the future at a lower price.

THE SCOOP

Why Hedge Funds are Different

CHAPTER 1

Distinguishing Characteristics

So now that you have reviewed some of the basic terminology in the industry, we will explain the key points in depth. The main distinguishing characteristics of hedge funds are the following:

• Hedge funds can "hedge" their portfolio
• Hedge funds use derivatives
• Hedge funds can purchase real assets, from real estate to entire companies
• Hedge funds can short sell
• Hedge funds have the ability to use leverage.

These characteristics make hedge funds different from most other investment funds, especially mutual funds. To get a good understanding of how a hedge fund manager operates, it is very important to understand these concepts. The four concepts are now defined in detail:

Hedging

Hedging refers to the execution of additional trades by the hedge fund manager in an attempt to counterbalance any risk involved with the existing positions in the portfolio. Hedging can be accomplished in many different ways, although the most basic technique is to purchase a long position and a secondary short position in a similar security (See Gap example). This is used to offset price fluctuations and is an effective way of neutralizing the effects of market conditions.

Hedging Example

Courtney is a hedge fund manager who invested in the Gap stores. Here we will see how he hedges his risk. Courtney is 'long' (he's bought) 100 shares of Gap Stores but he now believes the retail industry may be vulnerable to a down turn in the market. He wants to hedge this risk and does this by going "short" (selling) Abercrombie & Fitch, which is in the same retail industry.

Why Hedge Funds are Different

Q. What would happen if the retail industry did poorly?
A. The share prices of both Gap and Abercrombie & Fitch might decline.

Q. How would this affect any money Courtney makes?
A. Since Courtney is long on Gap (he owns it) he would lose money on this trade. Since Courtney is also short (he has already sold it) Abercrombie & Fitch, he would make money on that trade. Therefore he can offset some of his losses from Gap with gains from Abercrombie & Fitch. He reduces his risk of Gap by hedging with Abercrombie & Fitch.

Q. When you say Courtney gains from the Abercrombie & Fitch trade, what does this mean?
A. When Courtney goes short A&F it means he has sold it before he owns it. So say he sold 100 A&F shares short for $50 each. He receives $5,000 cash for doing so. This transaction is conducted through his broker and he now owes 100 A&F shares to his broker, to be paid back at some time the future. As time goes by the retail industry does poorly and the share price of A&F falls to $40.

Q. If the stock price of A&F falls to $40, what does this mean for Courtney's profits?
A. Since Courtney owes 100 A&F shares to his broker he can now go out and buy the 100 shares for $40 each, costing him a total of $4,000. Therefore Courtney has made $1,000 profit. (He received $5,000 from the original short sale and then paid $4,000 to buy A&F, so his profit is $1,000)

Derivatives

Derivatives that are used by hedge funds can take on many forms, and the more complex derivatives (interest rate swaps, foreign currency swaps, contract for differences, total return swaps, etc.) are not covered in this book. Discussed now are the most basic forms of derivatives: 'put' and 'call' options on stocks.

Option Definitions

Put option
A 'put' option gives the holder the right to sell the underlying stock at a specified price

Call option

A 'call' option gives the holder the right to buy the underlying stock at specified price (strike price) on or before a given date (exercise date).

Option writer

The seller of these options is referred to as the "writer"—many hedge funds will often write options in accordance with their strategies. This is the person who originates an option contract by promising to perform a certain obligation in return for the price or premium of the option. Any investor can sell options (write options) provided they have answered an options questionnaire provided to them by their broker. This would determine the knowledge of the investor and whether they understand the risks associated with writing options.

How does a hedge fund manager use options to reduce risk?

Consider Kristin, a long/short hedge fund manager, who in January 2004 owns 1,000 Wal-Mart shares. The current share price is $73 per share. Kristin is concerned about developments in Wal-Mart's illegal immigrant lawsuit that may cause the share price to decline sharply in the next two months and wants to protect herself from this risk. The process that Kristin would go through to hedge the risk of Wal-Mart's share price falling would be:

- Kristin could buy 10 July 'put' options with a strike price of $65 on the Chicago Board Options Exchange (www.cboe.com).

- This 'put' option gives Kristin the right to sell 1,000 shares for $65 per share at any time before it expires in July. If the market price of Wal-Mart falls below $65, the options can be exercised so that Kristin received $65,000 for the entire holding. When the cost of the options is taken into account, the amount realized is $62,500.

- If the quoted option price is $2.50, each option contract would cost $250. Since each option contract is valued per 100 shares, the total cost of the hedging strategy would be 10* $250 = $2,500.

- Although this strategy costs $2,500, it guarantees that the shares can be sold for at least $65 per share for the life of the option (it expires in July).

- But if the market price stays above $65, the options are not exercised because Kristin can make more money by just selling the shares for market price.

The Chicago Board Options Exchange (CBOE)

The CBOE created an orderly market with well-defined contracts on 16 stocks when it began trading call option contracts in 1973. The exchange began trading put options in 1977. The CBOE now trades options on over 1,200 stocks and many different stock indices. Many other exchanges throughout the world also trade option contracts. To learn more, visit the exchange's web site at www.cboe.com.

Real assets

Increasingly, hedge funds have purchased a variety of hard assets in their pursuit of returns. This involves buying something with a physical presence – anything from a Manhattan office building or a particular currency to an entire company. These assets are generally "flipped" – quickly sold so as to pocket a profit – or held for long-term income.

Examples of real asset investments

Sam's hedge fund joins an investment group that purchases an office building in downtown San Francisco, paying $10 million for a 50 percent stake. That building generates $2.5 million a year in leases after expenses. So Sam's stake generates $1.25 million a year for the fund. If he opts to sell his stake in three years, appreciating real estate prices may allow him to ask $12 million for the stake. So for three years' of leasing plus the profit on the sale, Sam has generated $5.75 million on a $10 million investment.

Lisa sees that the British pound is on the rise. She buys $10 million in pounds, which equals 5.151 pounds sterling. A few days later, she sees the dollar has fallen further. She reverses the trade, and brings in $10.25 million - a $250,000 profit in a matter of days.

Tim's team puts in $1 billion for a 25 percent stake in XYZ Corp., which is being taken private through a consortium of investors. Immediately, the investors lever the company by issuing $5 billion in bonds, half of which is used by the company for development, and half of which is given back to investors. Tim brings back $625 million of his stake within a few months. Two years later, the company is stronger than ever and the owners, Tim included, decide to take the company public again. The ensuing IPO values the company at $5 billion, and within two months, the overall value increases to $5.5 billion as the stock gathers steam. Tim still owns 25 percent of the company, which is now worth $1.375 billion. So in two years, Tim has made $1 billion on his investment - a 100 percent gain.

Short selling (going "short")

Short selling involves the selling of a security that the seller does not own. Short sellers believe that the stock price will fall and that they will be able to repurchase the stock at a lower price in the future. Thus, they will profit from selling the stock at a higher price, then buy it in the future at a lower price. (The opposite of going "short" is going "long," when investors buy stocks they believe will rise.)

Short Selling Example

Jimmy believes that McDonald's is overvalued and that he can profit by selling short "MCD." Jimmy sells short 100 shares at $50 which means he has sold stock that he does not yet own (this is a stock loan). In the future he has to buy the stock to repay the stock loan he entered into when shorting the stock. But, McDonald's price continues to rise to $75, which means that in order to buy the stock (this is called "covering" his stock loan), Jimmy pays $75 per share which results in his losing $2,500 (100 * $25).

Before Jimmy enters into the short sale, he must ensure that he is able to borrow the stock (get a stock loan), usually through its prime broker. Jimmy will call the stock loan department of the prime broker to see if the prime broker has the stock available to lend to him. If the stock loan department has the stock to lend, then Jimmy can short sell the stock (borrowing it from the prime broker). If the stock is not available for borrow, Jimmy cannot sell short the security.

Visit the Vault Finance Career Channel at **www.vault.com/finance** — with insider firm profiles, message boards, the Vault Finance Job Board and more.

V∆ULT CAREER LIBRARY

15

Leverage

Leverage measures the amount of assets being borrowed for each investment dollar. Leverage (borrowing additional funds) is utilized by hedge fund managers when they believe that the cost of the borrowed funds will be minimal compared to the returns of a particular position. It can be a key component to hedge fund management since it gives the hedge fund managers the ability to have higher returns (and potentially lose more) with borrowed funds.

Typical hedge fund leverage depends on the type of financial instruments that the hedge fund trades. Fixed income has lower risk levels so it is not uncommon to have four or five times the value of the fund borrowed. Equities have a higher risk profile and therefore typical leverage is one and a half to two times the value of the fund. However hedge funds are usually comprised of long and short positions, so a large market rise or fall has little impact if their profitable positions were equally balanced by their losing positions.

The simplest examples in everyday life of leverage are house mortgages and car loans. The bank manager uses the house or the car as collateral for the loan from the bank. The bank manager can then sell the house or the car if you default on your loan. Similarly, the hedge fund manager uses the financial instruments in his account as collateral for the funds he has borrowed from his bank (prime broker). The primary sources of leverage are financial institutions and banks. If the hedge fund manager cannot pay the loan back, the financial institution can then sell the collateral (the financial instruments in the account) to pay back the loan.

Leverage Calculation Example

If the hedge fund has $1 million of invested money and is borrowing another $2 million, to bring the total dollars invested to $3 million, then the leverage used is 200 percent. The amount of leverage typically used by the fund is shown as a percentage of the fund.

Hedge Funds vs. Mutual Funds

The closest cousin to hedge funds in the financial services world is the mutual fund. There are some similarities between the two, but there are several important differences as well.

What is a Mutual Fund?

A mutual fund is operated by an investment firm that raises money from shareholders and then invests in a group of assets (equities or fixed income). The mutual fund manager invests in accordance with a stated set of objectives (guidelines). The mutual funds raise money by selling shares of the fund to the public (usually there are very few stipulations on who can invest in the fund). Mutual fund managers then take the money they receive from the sale of their shares (along with any money made from previous investments) and use it to purchase various investment vehicles, such as stocks, bonds and money market instruments. Shareholders are free to sell their shares at any time.

Hedge funds differ from regular mutual funds because they have the ability to use leverage, sell short securities and use derivatives. Many hedge funds use short selling and/or derivatives to hedge their portfolio. Most mutual funds cannot use leverage, short sell or use derivatives. As mentioned previously, the term "hedging" refers to entering transactions that protect against adverse price movements.

Why Hedge Funds are Different

The following table highlights the main differences between hedge funds and mutual funds:

Characteristics	Hedge Funds	Mutual Funds
Asset classes (Type of investment, such as stocks, bonds, real estate, or cash)	Can use a wide variety of asset classes – stocks, cash, bonds, commodities, derivatives, currencies and hard assets.	Are usually limited to only using equities or bonds (The equity fund or bond fund.)

Visit the Vault Finance Career Channel at www.vault.com/finance — with insider firm profiles, message boards, the Vault Finance Job Board and more.

VAULT CAREER LIBRARY

17

Characteristics	Hedge Funds	Mutual Funds
Markets (The general term for the organized trading of stocks through exchanges. The main stock markets in the world are the NYSE, NASDAQ, London Stock Exchange, and Tokyo Stock Exchange.)	Varies. One manager's guidelines might say that they only invest in the U.S. markets, while others may specialize in emerging markets overseas. Global macro managers may leave their mandates open to any market and any investment that can generate returns.	Most mutual funds usually stick with one specific market, usually the U.S. If the fund focused on international stocks / bonds then the mandate would allow for a global or international fund.
Transparency (The amount of trading disclosure that hedge fund managers have to give to the SEC (Securities and Exchange Commission) and their investors.	Currently, hedge fund managers are not required to disclose security positions and balances to their investors and the SEC.	Mutual funds have to disclose their positions to the SEC on a frequent basis, at least every quarter.
Minimum investment levels	High, though they've declined as of late. Most hedge funds require at least $250,000 or more, with some requiring as much as $1 million to $10 million. Some, however, have lowered their minimums substantially – as low as $25,000 in some cases.	Low – most don't have a minimum requirement and if there is one, it is usually between $500 and $5,000.
Subscription periods (When can you get your money back).	Long – 1 to 3 years	Short – daily access, but subject to early withdrawal fees.

Characteristics	Hedge Funds	Mutual Funds
Manager compensation	Based on performance	Based on assets under management
Management investment in their own fund	High	Low
Benchmark	Absolute (always positive)	Relative to a benchmark – usually the S&P 500

These key characteristics of hedge funds are defined in detail in the sections below.

Free choice of asset classes

The term "asset class" means a type of instrument, such as stocks, bonds, real estate or cash. As an example, stocks are a separate asset class from bonds. Financial instruments are instruments that have some monetary value or they record a monetary transaction. Stocks, bonds, options and futures are all examples of financial instruments.

Free choice of asset classes means the type of asset categories that the hedge fund manager can and will invest in is usually very broad. The types of assets (stocks, bonds, cash, commodities, etc.) in which the hedge fund may invest are outlined in the investment mandate (fund prospectus) that is given to investors before they invest into the hedge fund. In addition, the investment mandate details the exact trading strategies that the hedge fund employs.

Most mutual funds use only bonds or only equities to generate returns, as stipulated by their investment mandate. In comparison, hedge funds mandates may allow a wider variety of asset classes: equities, debt, commodities and derivative products. Hedge funds can also trade in bank debt, currencies, and futures—the whole gamut of investment opportunities.

Not all hedge funds allow a wider variety of asset classes; long/short equity managers might restrict their investment mandate to strictly stocks (equities). Other hedge funds may allow stocks, interest rates swaps, currencies and commodities and literally have no asset class investment restrictions; an example would be global macro hedge funds. (A detailed description of the global macro strategy is outlined in the hedge fund strategy section.)

Visit the Vault Finance Career Channel at **www.vault.com/finance** — with insider firm profiles, message boards, the Vault Finance Job Board and more.

VAULT CAREER LIBRARY

19

Major Stock Markets/Indices

Dow Jones: This is a price-weighted average of 30 actively traded stocks, which are primarily selected from the industrials sector (hence the name Dow Jones "Industrial" Average). The 30 stocks are chosen by the editors of The Wall Street Journal (which is published by Dow Jones & Company), a practice that dates back to the beginning of the century.

FTSE (London): The Financial Times Stock Exchange 100 stock index, a market cap weighted index of stocks traded on the London Stock Exchange. The FTSE is similar to the S&P 500 in the U.S.

NASDAQ: The NASDAQ is a computerized system established by the NASD to facilitate trading by providing broker/dealers with current bid and ask price quotes on over-the-counter stocks and some listed stocks. The NASDAQ does not have a physical trading floor; instead, all trading on the NASDAQ exchange is done electronically over a network of computers and telephones.

Free choice of markets

"Markets" is the general term for the organized trading of stocks through stock exchanges (stock markets). The main stock markets in the world are the NYSE, NASDAQ, London Stock Exchange, and Tokyo Stock Exchange.

Free choice of markets means that many hedge funds do not focus on one specific stock market. Not limiting investment opportunities to one market gives hedge funds the option to act on investment opportunities throughout the world. Many hedge funds, like most mutual funds, will specify that they strictly focus on the

Nikkei: The Nikkei Index is an index of 225 leading stocks traded on the Tokyo Stock Exchange. The Nikkei Index is similar to the S&P 500 in the U.S.

NYSE: The New York Stock Exchange is the oldest and largest stock exchange in the U.S., located on Wall Street in New York City. The NYSE is responsible for setting policy, supervising member activities, listing securities, overseeing the transfer of member seats, and evaluating applicants. It traces its origins back to 1792, when a group of brokers met under a tree at the tip of Manhattan and signed an agreement to trade securities. The NYSE still uses a large trading floor to conduct its transactions.

U.S. markets (NYSE and NASDAQ) while global macro and international mutual funds will leave their mandate broad enough to allow them to invest in many markets (U.S., Europe, Asia and emerging markets). In recent years, more and more hedge funds have opted for a much broader mandate, allowing them to participate in private equity, leveraged buyouts, currency swaps and real estate investments. This allows the managers to invest where they see opportunity to profit.

Free choice of trading style/strategy

A "trading strategy" refers to the investment approach or the techniques used by the hedge fund manager to have positive returns on the investments.

In the past, most hedge funds choose to confine themselves to one specific strategy. (Strategies are explained in detail later.) Examples include the "statistical arbitrage" strategy or "long/short equity" strategy. These managers would detail in their investment mandate that the fund only invests in long/short equities or follows a statistical arbitrage model.

However, hedge funds have increasingly left their mandates vague to allow them to exploit opportunities when they become available or simply to change strategies. By having a broadly defined strategy, the manager could continue to generate returns for his investors given many different market conditions.

Example of a Broad Investment Mandate

A merger arbitrage manager may find that the deal market for mergers has dried up but that there are ample opportunities in the distressed debt market. If that manager had an investment mandate that restricted the fund to only pursuing a merger arbitrage strategy then the manager would not be able to take advantage of opportunities outside of that market. If the manager has an investment mandate that covers more than one strategy (i.e., includes distressed debt), he is then free to choose investments in the distressed debt market.

Transparency (or lack thereof)

"Transparency" refers to the amount of trading disclosure that hedge fund managers have to give to the SEC (Securities and Exchange Commission) and their investors. "Trading disclosure" refers to revealing actual trades, portfolio positions, performance and assets under management.

Mutual funds have to disclose their positions to the SEC on a frequent basis, at least every quarter. Currently, hedge fund managers are not required to disclose security positions and balances to their investors and the SEC. This lack of transparency within the hedge fund industry can be viewed both positively and negatively. Hedge fund managers tend to use proprietary trading strategies and attempt to exploit market inefficiencies before other managers discover them. Therefore, disclosing their positions/trades could compromise their strategy and result in other managers poaching their strategies or trading against them. Most hedge funds limit the disclosure of performance and asset size to existing and potential investors.

High minimum investment levels

To be classified as a private investment pool under SEC rules (thereby not having to be subject to the same reporting requirements as mutual funds), hedge funds must comply with regulatory restrictions on the type of investors and the number of investors who can invest in their fund.

Most hedge funds require a minimum investment of $250,000, and many require anywhere from $1 million to $5 million. While larger funds require at least $10 million as a minimum investment, some funds, especially newcomers, have lowered their investment requirements in order to attract more capital—some minimums today are as low as $25,000.

Long subscription periods

The subscription period (also known as the "lockup period") is the amount of time that the investor is required to keep the investment in the fund without withdrawal, typically one to two years. After the subscription period ends, the fund may accept quarterly or yearly redemption notices. A redemption notice is a letter from the investor stating his or her intent to withdraw money from the hedge fund. In comparison, mutual funds usually have daily liquidity, which means the subscription period is one day. Due to the complex nature and often illiquid trading strategies, hedge fund managers require investors to have long subscription periods.

The lengthy subscription period helps the hedge fund manager allocate the capital better so that they do not keep a large amount of cash un-invested just in case an investor decides to withdraw from the fund (also known as "redeeming" their investment). These long subscription periods are standard and allow hedge funds to better manage capital for long-term trading strategies.

Performance compensation

Hedge fund managers are compensated in two ways, with a performance fee and a management fee. These managers will likely share the performance fee with their staff to provide incentives for the analysts/traders/risk managers to pick the right investments. Both the performance and management fees are paid for by the investors from their assets in the fund.

- **Performance fees.** These are generally 20 percent to 25 percent of the fund's returns (performance) over a given period and are designed to align manager interests with their investors. Top-performing funds can have performance fees in the 30 percent to 40 percent range—but the fund generally has to be a consistent top performer for investors to put up with a manager taking such a cut.

- **General management fees.** These typically range from 1 percent—2 percent of assets under management. Management fees support the general upkeep of the hedge fund office (i.e., electricity, office space, trading technology and salaries).

Most hedge funds have settled on the "two and 20" fee structure—a 2 percent management fee and a 20 percent performance fee each year. Most funds set a return benchmark before the manager takes a performance fee. For example, if a fund's benchmark is 10 percent returns each year, and it only returns 9 percent, then no performance fee is assessed. If a manager gets to 12 percent returns, then the 20 percent performance fee is assessed, and the fund participant would see that 12 percent return lowered to 9.6 percent as the manager takes his cut.

High management investment

The majority of hedge fund managers invest a significant proportion of their own capital within their own fund. High personal investment aligns manager interests with those of their shareholders. Most potential investors look for whether the hedge fund managers have invested in their own fund and what proportion of net worth the manager has invested in the fund. High manager investment levels signal to investors that the manager believes in his/her strategy since they are willing to invest a significant proportion of their own capital in the fund.

Absolute benchmark

When mutual funds are evaluated on performance they are normally evaluated "relatively" against a benchmark. The benchmark is normally the S&P 500.

Mutual fund benchmark example

If the S&P 500 gained 5 percent in one year and the mutual fund manager gained 10 percent, then the manager beat his/her benchmark by 5 percent. Similarly, if the S&P declined 10 percent in one year and the mutual fund manager was down 5 percent, then the manager still beat the benchmark by 5 percent.

The last example highlights that investors still lost 5 percent despite the fact that the manager outperformed their benchmark.

In comparison, hedge fund managers are expected to achieve absolute returns. To get even more confusing, hedge funds are often referred to as "absolute return" funds. Absolute return refers to achieving positive returns no matter what the market conditions. If the markets are down 20 percent the hedge fund manager is still expected to achieve positive returns. This compares to mutual fund managers who are just expected to perform better than their benchmark, which is usually the S&P 500. Therefore if the mutual fund manager is down 15 percent when the market is down 20 percent, he/she has performed better than the benchmark and is perceived to have done well for his/her investors. In contrast, hedge fund managers are expected to return a positive number at all times.

> An "absolute return" manager is one without a benchmark who is expected to achieve positive returns no matter what market conditions.

Hedge fund managers are able to short sell or use options to hedge risk so they should be able to avoid or take advantage of market downturns. Therefore, if the S&P gained or lost 10 percent, hedge funds should still deliver positive returns. Because hedge funds are not required to report performance publicly, there are few benchmarks that hedge funds can be compared against. Even within the same strategy, hedge funds have very different styles and, thus, are difficult to compare to one another.

Hedge Funds 101

CHAPTER 2

History of Hedge Funds

In 1949 Alfred W. Jones established the first hedge fund-type structure when he borrowed funds (used leverage) to increase his long positions while adding a portfolio of short stocks in an investment fund with an incentive fee structure. Carol J. Loomis used the term "hedge fund" in her 1966 Fortune magazine article where she discussed the structure and investment strategy used by Jones. Jones had set up his pool of investors as a limited partnership and was, thus, able to avoid the reporting requirements to which mutual funds were subjected. What drew Fortune's attention to Jones was that his fund significantly outperformed traditional investments. From 1960-1965 Jones' investments returned 325 percent while the Fidelity mutual fund returned 225 percent. During the 10-year period from 1955-1965 Jones' fund returned 670 percent compared to the Dreyfuss fund, which only returned 358 percent.

After the Fortune article, other money managers found Jones' investment style both profitable and intriguing and, thus, a growth spurt in the hedge fund industry began. In an attempt to copy Jones' style (and hopefully performance), many money managers began selling short securities without prior experience. Haphazard short selling by new hedge fund managers adversely affected their performance during the bull market of the mid-late 1960s. These hedge fund managers were not actually "hedging" their positions at all; they were leveraged to the long side of the portfolio (betting that the market would go up), which was particularly risky entering the bear markets of the 70s (when the markets declined). .

Bull market: A time in which the prices of stock in the market are rising or are expected to rise.

Bear market: A time in which the prices of stock in the market are falling or are expected to fall.

According to Alexander Ineichen in his book Absolute Returns, these managers produced substantial losses in 1969-70 and a major bloodletting ensued in the 1973-74 bear market. Ineichen's book is one of the most recommended books for those interested in learning in more depth about the hedge fund industry and its strategies.

The more experienced hedge fund managers survived the 1970s bear market. But, unfortunately many other hedge fund managers closed the doors. According to Gabelli in 1984, when Sandra Manske formed Tremont Partners and began researching the hedge fund industry, she was only able to identify 68 funds. It is hard to determine an exact figure for the funds at this time due to the lack of marketing and public registration.

Ineichen also states that the hedge fund industry remained relatively small until the early 1990s, when the financial press once again highlighted the returns achieved by hedge fund superstars George Soros (Quantum Fund) and Julian Robertson (Tiger Fund and its offshore sister, Jaguar Fund). What differed about this new growth of hedge fund managers was that the hedge fund managers added a variety of trading strategies, including the infamous global macro strategy pursued by George Soros.

Soros traded in the currency markets by buying and selling various currencies and most notably made over $1 billion betting against the British pound. Robertson employed modern financial derivatives such as futures and options, which didn't exist when Jones started his fund.

> Global macro is a hedge fund strategy that seeks to profit by making leveraged bets on anticipated price movements of global stock markets, interest rates, foreign exchange rates, and physical commodities.

The ability to use futures, options, swaps and other complex derivatives led to an explosion in the number of trading strategies. These strategies are not allowed to be employed in the mutual fund industry. Therefore, managers who felt that they could exploit the markets using these tools had to set up hedge funds. At the end of 1999, Tremont Partners estimated as many as 4,000 hedge funds existed, 2,600 of which were tracked in its database.

Estimates show that there were 300 hedge funds in existence in 1990. By 2000 that number had increased to 3,000 and by 2003 there were reported to be over 6,000 hedge funds. According to Hal Lux, the doubling of the number of hedge funds over the past three years has been due to the ability of hedge funds to outperform traditional markets in the recent bear market and investors' increased interest in the advanced trading strategies that they employ. The growth in the hedge fund industry also stems from increased interest in the industry from institutional investors (pension funds and endowments) and from the number of hedge fund managers entering the industry. Between 1992 and 2000 the institutional investor's share of the overall hedge fund market increased 147 percent.

Between the first and second editions of this career guide, the number of hedge funds has once again exploded, with estimates ranging between 7,000 and 8,000 funds globally. According to Hedge Fund Research Inc., hedge funds control some $1.3 trillion in assets. That's still a tenth of what the mutual fund industry controls, but that doesn't take away from hedge funds' massive growth and their increasing ability to directly affect the overall markets through the sheer weight of assets they can invest.

This growth has come even as the hedge fund industry experienced its first real regulatory crunch. In 2006, the U.S. Securities and Exchange Commission required hedge funds to register as investment advisors. The move, considered a compromise between funds and the SEC, allows for oversight of funds—including random checks of a given fund's accounting, for example—without requiring disclosures of holdings, strategies, past investments or other things that could ultimately give a fund's competitors a look into a fund's direction.

Structure of Hedge Funds

Hedge funds have private investment pools and can have legal entities onshore (United States) or offshore (Caribbean tax havens).

Onshore entity

This is typically set up as a limited partnership. The general partner of the limited partnership can be an entity or individuals, and in most circumstances is the fund manager, who may or may not have a portion of personal assets invested in the fund. The limited partners have limited liability depending on how much is invested in the partnership interest. General partners have unlimited liability since they assume legal responsibility for the hedge fund and thus could be subject to lawsuits.

Offshore entity

This is typically a corporation or other investment company forms (limited liability company or limited company) established in tax havens such as the Cayman Islands, Bermuda and British Virgin Islands. The offshore entity does not have a general partner to manage the limited partnership; instead it has a management company. Due to tax implications, generally the investors in the offshore funds are non-U.S. residents.

Because hedge funds are private, they are exempt from registering with the Securities and Exchange Commission (SEC). The privatization of hedge funds also regulates the number and type of investors allowed.

As mentioned previously, onshore and offshore hedge funds do not typically disclose all contents of their portfolios to their investors. A more recent trend is the increase in information (transparency) that is being demanded by investors; some portfolio information is being disclosed to these investors by hedge fund managers. This access to portfolio information by the investor is referred to as "transparency," which was previously discussed in depth.

Who Invests in Hedge Funds?

Hedge fund investors are traditionally wealthy individuals and family offices, pensions, endowments and institutions.

Pension

A pension is the post-retirement benefits that an employee might receive from some employers. A pension is essentially compensation received by the employee after he/she has retired. Possibly the largest pension fund is CalPERS. The California Public Employees' Retirement System (CalPERS) provides retirement and health benefit services to more than 1.5 million members and nearly 2,500 employers. CalPERS' total assets were over $230 billion at the end of 2006.

Endowment

An endowment is a permanent fund bestowed upon an individual or institution, such as a university, museum, hospital, or foundation, to be used for a specific purpose. Harvard, Yale, Stanford and the University of Texas are the largest four endowments. Due in part to increasing hedge fund investments, 62 American universities now boast billion-dollar endowments. In 2006, total assets of the top four endowments assets were reported to be:

• Harvard University: $28.9 billion

• Yale University: $ 18.0 billion

• Stanford University: $14.1 billion

• The University of Texas: $13.2 billion

Accredited investors and qualified purchasers

"Accredited investors" and "qualified purchasers" are the two types of investors that can invest in hedge funds. (More detailed explanations are found in the glossary.) The SEC defines "accredited investors" as individuals who have a net worth in excess of $1 million or income in excess of $200,000 individually or $300,000 when income is combined with a spouse. Qualified purchasers are entities that both hold and control $25 million in investments and also individuals or families or companies with $5 million in investments. Therefore only wealthy individuals, families and companies with large amount of investments can invest in hedge funds.

In recent years, however, hedge funds have been able to play around with this rule by attempting to operate under different regulatory rules, offering themselves as limited partnerships with their investors. For example, the Grenada-based Superfund requires a minimum of just $5,000, though investors must also meet income and net-asset requirements (which are generally easily attainable for most middle-class American families).

Visit the Vault Finance Career Channel at **www.vault.com/finance** — with insider firm profiles, message boards, the Vault Finance Job Board and more.

VAULT CAREER LIBRARY

29

Marketing and Hedge Funds

Getting information about a hedge fund used to be difficult for the average investor, but not anymore. The SEC prohibits marketing to unaccredited investors, which means hedge funds can't give out any performance information. Yet on any given day, CNBC and Bloomberg TV commercials tout hedge funds. While these commercials don't give any kind of performance metrics, they serve to put the name of the fund out there into the public consciousness. From there, would-be hedge fund investors are driven to the Internet or to their financial advisors with the name in hand. It's the same kind of advertising that pharmaceutical companies have used to skirt FDA regulations—don't make any claims, but get the name out there so you can ask your doctor.

While most hedge funds do not have Web sites, more of them have come online. Again, there's very little information available on actual performance on the Internet, but these sites again serve to whet the appetites of the individual investor. The sites also serve a dual purpose in allowing current investors or pre-qualified investors to access more detailed information about the fund.

Nonetheless, hedge fund marketing remains highly targeted. Hedge funds approach pension funds, endowments, major corporations, private banks and investment banks—entities that are assured of being qualified investors. Private wealth managers—in particular, have increasingly invested their clients' money in hedge funds, given that the majority of their clients are indeed likely to qualify.

Hedge fund managers still speak at major hedge fund and investor conferences, and word-of-mouth still has a place. But slowly and surely, hedge funds have been cautiously expanding their marketing efforts, ensuring they reach every potential investor they can.

How Hedge Fund Managers Make Money

So how do all these hedge funds make money? In addition to the 1 to 2 percent management fees that the hedge funds charge investors, managers also make significant money from performance fees generated by their funds. Performance fees can range from 15 percent to 50 percent, with 20 percent increasingly becoming the industry standard. Performance fees aren't charged in months or years when the fund does not generate a profit. They're also usually constrained by high water marks.

High Water Marks

A high water mark means if the fund loses money in one year or time period, then the limited partner's (investor's) capital account has to get back to that high water mark (the high point of value that the fund/account was at) before the manager starts getting a performance percentage share of new appreciation.

For example, say Peter invested $10 million into Hedge Fund Manager A in Year 0. Say Hedge Fund Manager A performed poorly and lost 10 percent, leaving Peter's investment valued at $9 million at the end of Year 1. For this year, there would be no performance fee charged. Moreover, Hedge Fund Manager A must bring Peter's investment above the high water mark of $10 million in Year 2 before he can begin charging a performance fee.

Hedge fund managers are typically compensated based on their performance by getting a percentage, usually 20 percent, of the gains made by the fund. If the fund has a hurdle, this means the fund has to gain that much—the amount of the hurdle—before the hedge fund manager starts sharing in the profits. Say a fund has a 10 percent hurdle, and the manager charges a 20 percent performance allocation. If the fund only makes 10 percent in a year, the manager gets no share because the fund has not exceeded the hurdle. If the fund makes 20 percent one year, then that year the manager would take the 20 percent return, subtract the 10 percent hurdle, and get 20 percent (the performance fee) of the 10 percent that is left.

Visit the Vault Finance Career Channel at www.vault.com/finance — with
insider firm profiles, message boards, the Vault Finance Job Board and more.

VAULT CAREER LIBRARY   31

Hedge Fund Strategies

Hedge fund managers utilize a variety of complex and interesting trading strategies. There are many different ways for managers to value stocks but this is beyond the scope of this book. (There are many great books on investment theory that cover in detail how managers and analysts value securities; see the Appendix of this book for recommendations.)

Here is a basic overview of the valuation process that a hedge fund manager or analyst goes through in picking stocks to invest in.

Valuation Process

When an analyst is looking to value a company (to determine what he thinks should be the correct stock price) he goes through a process to determine what he believes the stock price to be. This is similar to the process of buying new clothes or buying a car or house when you figure out how much it is worth to you and how much you are willing to pay. You are looking for the best deal available—if a price is above what you are willing to pay, you do not buy the product; if the price is below what you are willing to pay, you do buy it.

According to Reilly and Brown in their book *Investment Analysis and Portfolio Management*, there are two basic approaches to valuing stocks: the "top down" and the "bottom up" process:

(1) The "top down" (three step) process

The manager believes that the economy, the stock market and the industry all have a significant effect on the total returns for stocks

The three-step process is:

i. Analysis of alternative economies and security markets. Decide how to allocate investment funds among countries and within countries to bonds, stocks and cash

ii. Analysis of alternative industries. Decide based upon the economic and market analysis, determine which industries will prosper and which will suffer on a global basis and within countries.

iii. Analysis of individual companies and stocks. Following the selection of the best industries, determine which companies within these industries will prosper and which stocks are under/over valued.

(2) The "bottom up" (stock valuation, stock picking) approach

a. Investors who employ the bottom up stock picking approach believe that it is possible to find stocks that are under and overvalued, and that these stocks will provide superior returns, regardless of market conditions

How to value these assets?

Without going into the complex valuation methodologies, the basic process of valuation requires estimates of (1) the stream of expected returns and (2) the required rate of return in the investment. Once the analyst has calculated these expected returns he can then compute his expected value of the stock.

The hedge fund trading strategies aim to maximize investor return while hedging market risk. Let's now take a look at these strategies in detail.

Fixed Income Arbitrage

Fixed income arbitrage (also known as relative value arbitrage) involves taking long and short positions in bonds and other interest rate-sensitive securities. The positions could include corporate debt, sovereign debt, municipal debt, swaps and futures.

Ineichen describes the fixed income manager as one who invests in related fixed income securities whose prices are mathematically or historically interrelated but the hedge fund manager believes this relationship will soon change. Because the prices of these fixed income instruments are based on yield curves, volatility curves, expected cash flows and other option features, the fixed income managers use sophisticated analytical models to highlight any potential trading opportunities. When these sophisticated models highlight relationships of two or more bonds that are out of line, the manager will buy the undervalued security and sell the overvalued security.

Fixed income arbitrage trading example

Callie is a fixed income hedge fund manager. Her analytical model highlights that the spread of the T-bill/Eurodollar contracts is 120 basis points. Callie believes that this spread is going to widen since she believes that the Eurodollar futures contracts are overvalued.

Callie enters into two trades:

	Beg price	End price	Profits
Buys 10 T-bill futures contracts @	94.30	94.25	($12.50)
(Sell T-Bill contracts @ 94.25 (loss of 5 basis points * $25 per basis point * 10 contracts)			
Sells short 10 Eurodollar futures contracts @	93.10	92.95	$37.50
(Buy 10 Eurodollar contracts @ 92.95 = 15 basis points * $25 per basis point * 10 contracts)			

Callie's analysis proved correct when the spread widened to 130 basis points and she made a profit of $2,500.

Convertible Arbitrage

Convertible arbitrage encompasses very technical and advanced hedging strategies. At its simplest, the hedge fund manager has bought (and holds) a convertible bond and has sold short the overvalued underlying equities of the same issuer. The manager identifies pricing inefficiencies between the convertible bond and stock and trades accordingly.

Visit the Vault Finance Career Channel at **www.vault.com/finance** — with
insider firm profiles, message boards, the Vault Finance Job Board and more.

VAULT CAREER LIBRARY

35

Convertible arbitrage trading example

Heather is a convertible arbitrage manager; she trades her strategy by establishing a short position in the stock that the bond can be converted into. This practice, known as delta hedging, consists of dividing the price of the convertible by the stock price conversion premium and then multiplying by the option delta. Heather buys $1 million Lyondell Chemical Corp convertible bond at 95¾ and sells short 20,000 of Lyondell Chemical company stock. The bond positions were sold at 101½ and the common equity was covered at a loss at $14.43. Even though the short position produced a loss of $18,400, the bonds made $65,521. Overall, Heather made a profitable trade with an overall gain of $47,121.

	Quantity	Purchase price	Ending Price	Total Return
Long – 9 5/8% Sr Sec Nts due 5/1/07	$1.0 mm	95¾	101½	$65,521
Short – Common Equity	20,000 shs	$13.51	$14.43	$(18,400)
				NET $47,121

Statistical Arbitrage

Statistical arbitrage encompasses a variety of sophisticated strategies that use quantitative models to select stocks. The hedge fund manager buys undervalued stocks and sells short overvalued stocks. This is also referred to as the "black box" strategy since computer models make many of the trading decisions for the hedge fund manager.

Statistical arbitrage example

Suzi is a statistical arbitrage manager at QuantHedge working with a team of quantitative analysts who all hold Ph.D.s in physics or mathematics. The team at QuantHedge has developed a computer-generated mathematical model that picks a large basket of stocks to buy and a separate basket to short based on parameters. The model is used to help predict where the market is going and whether a stock is over- or under-priced. The model uses various data as inputs (historical stock prices, liquidity, pricing inefficiencies, etc.) and these are set forth by the manager.

Based on the imputs, the QuantHedge model generates automatic buy or sell orders. Suzi monitors what the model is doing and notices that the model "HedgeIt" shows AT&T usually trades at $20 and has recently risen to $24. HedgeIt's analysis predicts that the AT&T is overvalued and automatically generates a sell order. These computer models generate hundreds and thousands of trade orders each day.

Equity Market Neutral

The most popular statistical arbitrage strategy is equity market neutral. An equity market neutral strategy (also known as statistical arbitrage) involves constructing portfolios that consist of approximately equal dollar amounts of offsetting long and short positions. The equity market neutral strategy is one that attempts to eliminate market risk by balancing long and short positions equally, usually offsetting total dollar amount of long positions with an equal dollar position amount of short positions. Net exposure to the market is reduced because if the market moves dramatically in one direction, gains in long positions will offset losses in short positions, and vice versa. If the long positions that were selected are undervalued and the short positions were overvalued, there should be a net benefit.

Equity market neutral trading example

Adam is an equity market neutral hedge fund manager. He tries to eliminate market risk by balancing long and short positions equally. He normally uses futures to totally eliminate market risk but here is an example where he balances the long and short equity in the portfolio. Adam believes that shares of ABC are overvalued and XYZ are undervalued and hopes to offset any dramatic market movements by holding offsetting equity (total value of longs—total value of shores) positions.

	Beg price	End price	Profits
Adam sells short 500 shares of ABC	$10	$11	($500)
Adam buys 200 shares of XYZ	$25	$30	$1000
Net dollar position is		($0)	$500

Although Adam was wrong on ABC's price declining, he was correct about XYZ appreciating. Therefore, he made an overall profit of $500.

Long/Short Equity

Long/short equity strategies involve taking both long and short positions in equity. Unlike market neutral portfolios, long/short equity portfolios will generally have some net market exposure, usually in the long direction. This means that managers are "long biased" when they have more exposure to long positions than short. Long/short fund managers may operate with certain style biases such as value or growth approaches and capitalization or sector concentrations.

Long/short trading example

Denver is a long/short equity hedge fund manager whose primary trading strategy focuses on sector trades. After conducting analysis of the financial condition of GM and Ford, Denver notices that in the automotive sector, GM is a relatively cheap stock when compared with Ford. Denver purchases 100 shares of GM because GM is undervalued relative to the theoretical price (what Denver calculates) and the stock market is expected to correct the price. Simultaneously, Denver sells short 100 shares of Ford because Ford is overvalued relative to its theoretical price according to Denver's fundamental analysis.

	Beg price	End price	Profits
By 100 shares of GM @	55	60	500
Sell short 100 shares of Ford @	15	14	100
Total			$600

Denver predicted that the price of GM would rise and the price of Ford would fall. He was correct and made a total profit of $600.

Distressed Securities (High Yield)

Distressed investing strategies consist of investing in companies that are experiencing financial difficulties—possible bankruptcies. These companies are usually priced very low due to the risk of default—most mutual funds cannot invest in companies whose credit ratings fall below secure—therefore these hedge funds can take advantage of very low prices.

Distressed debt example

Jane works for a distressed debt hedge fund manager. As an analyst it is her responsibility to evaluate low-grade debt and calculate the probability that it will pay more when it matures. Jane notices that the low-grade high-yield bonds for AlmostBankrupt Inc are trading for 20 percent to 30 percent of par value. This means that Jane would pay 20 to 30 cents on the dollar for the AlmostBankrupt Inc, bond. After careful evaluation, Jane believes that the bonds will appreciate or have a high percentage chance of paying full par at maturity.

	Price buy	Sell	Total
Buy: AlmostBankrupt Inc bonds	20	25	5

Jane was correct and when she decided to sell, the bonds were selling for 25 percent more at 25 cents on the dollar. But Jane sees that many of these bonds won't pay off the full par value. By constructing a diversified portfolio of high yield bonds the manager reduces the risk of the portfolio through diversification.

Commodities

Increasingly, hedge funds have been investing in commodities. Indeed, hedge funds were blamed for the sharp 2005 increase in natural gas futures—and the subsequent burst bubble in 2006 that prompted Amaranth Advisors LLC to go out of business. Most of the time, hedge funds simply see commodity trading as yet another tool for hedging against risk and increasing returns. They trade commodity

Visit the Vault Finance Career Channel at www.vault.com/finance — with insider firm profiles, message boards, the Vault Finance Job Board and more.

VAULT CAREER LIBRARY

39

futures much like any other investor. Hedge funds' success in commodities trading in the first half of the decade prompted major investment firms like Merrill Lynch and Morgan Stanley to bolster their own energy trading operations.

Currencies

Hedge funds have taken to playing the currency markets as another way to find alpha. Investing in foreign equities or bonds often require that investment to be made in local currency. In a good investment, the fund will not only see returns based on the investment itself, but also in a beneficial exchange rate.

In recent years, hedge funds and other investors have also used the carry trade to boost returns. In this scenario, a hedge fund hoping to leverage a trade will borrow money from a bank in a country that has a low interest rate—Japan has been a particular favorite in the past few years. With the benchmark rate in the U.S. at 5 percent and Japan's at 1 percent, that generally means a 400-basis-point difference.

Currencies example

For example, CarryTrade Hedge Fund wants to buy up Company XYZ stock and use leverage to do so. It has $10 million and wants to borrow another $40 million in leverage. If it were to borrow in the U.S., it might have to pay 10 percent on the loan, or $4 million. But in Japan, the loan only has 6 percent interest, or $2.4 million. So on top of whatever profit it makes on the trade, the fund saves $1.6 million in interest. And if it plays its cards right, it can also gain a few hundred thousand dollars by timing the currency market right.

Private Equity

As mentioned previously, hedge funds are playing an increasingly important role in taking companies private. At times they partner with more traditional private equity firms, while other times they'll buy up the bonds used as leverage in the buyout, or even directly extend credit to the buyers in exchange for a stake in the company. The returns are generally longer-term than most hedge funds are used to, so only the biggest hedge funds generally engage in any private equity plays.

Real Estate

Hedge funds have increasingly invested in hard assets, particularly real estate. Commercial real estate, in particular, has remained strong despite the downturn in the residential housing market in the United States. Commercial leasing can provide steady returns for hedge funds, which can hedge against risks in other markets. And commercial real estate has generally appreciated in value far more consistently than residential holdings.

Event-Driven

An "event-driven" fund is a fund that utilizes an investment strategy that seeks to profit from special situations or price fluctuations. Various styles or strategies may be simultaneously employed. Strategy may be changed as deemed appropriate – there is no commitment to any particular style or asset class. The manager invests both long and short in equities or fixed income of companies that are expected to change due to an unusual event.

Event-driven example

Rob is an event-driven manager who invests in companies that are going through various restructures. Rob and his team at EventsRUs hedge fund analyze many company balance sheets and research industries to find any news that could affect the price of the companies' stocks. These events include: corporate restructurings (mergers, acquisitions, and spin-offs), stock buy-backs, bond upgrades, and earnings surprises.

Rob has noticed that the market is predicting poor sales for AutoZone (AZO) for the fourth quarter. Rob has researched the company and noticed that while the industry is doing well, other analysts are not pricing in price improvements. He therefore makes a decision to buy AZO under the premise that they will surprise at earnings and the stock price will go up.

	Beg	End	Profit
Buy: 100 AZO	85	90	$500

Rob was correct and makes a profit of $500 on the trade.

Visit the Vault Finance Career Channel at **www.vault.com/finance** — with
insider firm profiles, message boards, the Vault Finance Job Board and more.

VAULT CAREER LIBRARY

41

Sector

Sector strategies invest in a group of companies/segment of the economy with a common product or market. The strategy combines fundamental financial analysis with industry experience to identify best profit opportunities in the sector. Examples could be the health care, technology, financial services or energy sectors.

Sector example

Richard is a long/short equity hedge fund manager whose primary trading strategy focuses on sector trades. Richard notices that in the financials sector Bear Stearns (BSC) is a relatively cheap stock when compared with JP Morgan (JPM). Richard purchases 100 shares of BSC because BSC is undervalued relative to the theoretical price (fair value) and the market is expected to correct the price. Simultaneously, Richard sells short 100 shares of JPM because JPM is overvalued relative to its theoretical price.

	Beg price	Sell price	Profits
Buy 100 shares of BSC @	85	90	500
Sell short 100 shares of JPM @	40	39	100
Total			$600

Richard predicted that the price of Bear Stearns would rise and the price of JP Morgan would fall. He was correct and made a total profit of $600.

Global Macro

Global macro is a style of hedge fund strategy that trades based upon macro economic or "top-down" analysis. Normally the securities are global stock index futures, bond futures, and currencies.

Global macro trading example

The classic example of this trading style is the trade that George Soros made against the British pound in 1992. He shorted over 10 billion pounds forecasting that the British government would allow the pound to break the EMS "bands" (fixed exchange rate mechanism tying the pound to the deutsche mark) dictated at the time. At the time, Britain's economy was struggling because of high interest rates that were necessary to keep the pound/mark exchange rate within the Bundesbank restrictions of the European monetary system. On Black Wednesday in Sept 1992, the British government (after spending billions of pounds in foreign currency reserves to support the pound) allowed the pound to fall out of the EMS. Soros reportedly made more than $1 billion as the price of the pound declined rapidly.

The global macro manager constructs his portfolio based on a macro top-down view of the global economic trends. He/she will consider interest rates, economic policies, exchange rates, inflation etc., and seek to profit from changes in the value of entire asset classes. An example of a trade would be to purchase U.S. dollar futures while shorting Eurodollar futures. By doing this, a hedge fund manager is indicating that he believes that the U.S. dollar is undervalued but the Eurodollar is overvalued.

Short Selling

The short selling manager maintains a consistent net short exposure in his/her portfolio, meaning that significantly more capital supports short positions than is invested in long positions (if any is invested in long positions at all). Unlike long positions, which one expects to rise in value, short positions are taken in those securities the manager anticipates will decrease in value. Short selling managers typically target overvalued stocks, characterized by prices they believe are too high given the fundamentals of the underlying companies.

Short selling trading example

Amy is a trader for a hedge fund that focuses primarily on short selling. During the late 1990s dot-com bubble there were many opportunities for short selling tremendously overpriced securities. Amy sold short Yahoo

(YHOO) at $60 and has maintained the position until today. She has made a handsome profit since Yahoo currently trades at $48.

	Sell	Buy	Profit
Sell short 1,000 YHOO	$60	$48	$12,000

Amy believes that the companies that are prime examples for short selling are those whose stock market values greatly exceed their fundamental values.

Emerging Markets

Emerging market investing involves investing in securities issued by businesses and/or governments of countries with less developed economies that have the potential for significant future growth.

Emerging markets example

A manager would trade equities and fixed income in lesser-developed countries (or emerging nations/markets) including Brazil, China, India, and Russia. Most emerging market countries are located in Latin America, Eastern Europe, Asia, or the Middle East. An example of this would be to trade long the Chinese yuan (CNY) and short the HK dollar (HKD), believing that the yuan will appreciate relative to the HKD.

Merger Arbitrage

Merger arbitrage involves the investing of event-driven situations of corporations; examples are leveraged buy-outs, mergers, and hostile takeovers. Managers purchase stock in the firm being taken over and, in some situations, sell short the stock of the acquiring company.

Merger arbitrage trading example

Mike is a merger arbitrage hedge fund manager following a potential merger between Company A and Company B.

Mike offers one share of Company A, trading at $105, for each share of Company B stock, currently trading at $80. Following the merger announcement, Company B's stock rises to $100 per share. Mike buys Company stock B at $100 and sells short Company A shares at $105 in an equal to the exchange ratio—in this case 1-to-1. As the merger date approaches, the $5 spread will narrow as the prices of Company B and Company A stocks converge. When the spread narrows, Mike's profits grow—for example, if Company B stock rises to $101 and Company A falls to $98, Mike earns $1 on Company B (the long investment) and $7 on Company A (the short).

Mike's risk is that the deal will not go through and Company B's share price will drop back to $80 resulting in a substantial loss for him.

Value-Driven

Value-driven is a primarily equity-based strategy whereby the manager compares the price of a security relative to the intrinsic worth of the underlying business. The manager often selects stocks for which he or she can identify a potential upcoming event that will result in the stock price changing to more accurately reflect the company's intrinsic worth.

Value-driven example

Tom is a value-focused hedge fund manager. He pores through the accounting statements of the companies that he invests in and visits executives at many of them. He focuses on companies in the retail sector; because of his industry focus, he is also actually able to visit stores and even speak to the staff working at the company. After extended research, Tom feels that company XYZ is undervalued (i.e., the stock price is low given company fundamentals such as high earnings per share, good cash flow, strong management, etc.) and ABC is overvalued (i.e. the stock price is too high given the company's fundamentals).

	Purchase price	Sell price	Profit
Tom purchases 100 shares of XYZ @	$40	$45	$500
Tom sells short 50 shares of ABC @	$80	$78	$100

Tom's valuation was correct and he made a total profit of $600

Multi-Strategy

A multi-strategy manager typically utilizes two or three specific, predetermined investment strategies, e.g., value, aggressive growth, and special situations. This gives the investor access to multiple strategies with one investment. These funds also allow the manager to shift between strategies so that he can make the most money. This is similar to a situation in which a merger arbitrage manager left his investment mandate broad enough so that he could invest in distressed debt if the opportunity arose. Multi-strategy funds can offset some of the risk of one strategy doing poorly by employing other strategies simultaneously.

Fund of Hedge Funds (Fund of Funds)

A fund of hedge funds is also a hedge fund. This strategy invests in other hedge funds, which in turn utilize a variety of investment styles. A fund of funds takes investments from various investors and invests the money into a variety of different hedge funds. This allows for diversification of strategies and markets and increased chance of positive returns with low risk.

Like other hedge funds, funds of funds are organized as onshore or offshore entities that are limited partnership or corporations with the general partner receiving the management and/or performance fee.

Funds of funds can offer an effective way for an investor to gain exposure to a range of hedge funds and strategies without having to commit substantial assets or resources to the specific asset allocation, portfolio construction and individual hedge fund selection. The objective is to smooth out the potential inconsistency of the returns from having all of the assets invested in a single hedge fund.

A growing number of style or category specific funds of funds have been launched during the past few years; for example, funds of funds that invest only in event-driven managers or funds of funds that invest only in equity market neutral style managers.

The funds of hedge funds now control roughly 35 to 40 percent of the hedge fund market and have grown at up to 40 percent every year since 1997. This allocation creates a diverse vehicle and provides investors with access to managers that they may not be able to utilize on their own. A particular benefit of this type of investment is the ability to establish a diversified alternative investment program at a substantially lower minimum investment than would be required were an investor to invest with each of the hedge fund managers separately.

Headliners and Legends: Major Hedge Funds

CHAPTER 4

Long-Term Capital Management

Hedge funds have become famous in recent years for their impressive returns and one or two interesting scandals, but most hedge fund managers do not make the headlines. Hedge fund managers are usually very talented individuals with numerous years of investment experience with major investment banks. Gary Weiss and Joseph Weber answered the mystery question of who hedge fund managers actually are: "They are, for the most part, veteran Wall Streeters who have decided to go into business for themselves—investing their own money and the funds of a handful of clients and receiving in return a hefty portion of the profit."

If you're interested in a hedge fund career, you should be familiar with the story of Long-Term Capital Management, which in 1998 almost brought down the world's financial markets, lost over $4 billion and was bailed out by the major Wall Street firms concerned about the stability of world financial markets. If you haven't read it, the story is incredible and explained brilliantly in Roger Lowenstein's *When Genius Failed: The Rise and Fall of Long-Term Capital Management*.

As probably the most infamous hedge fund in history, Long-Term Capital Management (LTCM) was built on pure genius. The founding partners of LTCM included John Meriwether, the legendary king of Salomon Brothers bond trading on Wall Street and Robert Merton and Myron Scholes, Nobel laureates in economics who (together with the late Fischer Black) all but invented modern finance through their theory on pricing options. Between 1994 and April 1998, LTCM seemed invincible. At its peak it had $130 billion under management and a derivatives portfolio with a notional value of $7 trillion dollars (equivalent to the entire annual budget of the U.S. government).

Then it all went wrong, and very wrong indeed. The assumptions buried in Scholes and Merton's theory on option pricing began to break down and, during that fateful summer of 1998, this breakdown was further aggravated by the collapse of the Russian market. LTCM was highly leveraged and made

Visit the Vault Finance Career Channel at **www.vault.com/finance** — with insider firm profiles, message boards, the Vault Finance Job Board and more.

VAULT CAREER LIBRARY

49

some of its trades based on the price relationship between corporate and government bonds. The Russian market collapse meant that there was a flight to quality from corporate to government bonds, when LTCM's model had predicted the reverse. This market collapse, along with more highly leveraged merger arbitrage trades that performed poorly, meant that LTCM's performance was disastrous. In August 1998, the fund was down 44 percent and on August 21, 1998, the fund lost a staggering $550 million.

We'll repeat that for emphasis: In one day, the fund lost $550 million!

So what happened to cause this infamous meltdown? Let's take a look at the pivotal events during 1998 that led up to LTCM's meltdown

1998 chronology of events

Following a successful 1997, LTCM returned $2.7 billion to outside investors. It then began the year with $4.8 billion in capital invested in the fund.

Through April, the fund was up 2.4 percent before fees.

May and June were the worst months ever for LTCM. The fund returned -6.7 percent and -10.1 percent respectively.

Near the end of June, LTCM's principals decided to reduce the some of the positions in the portfolio, which would make the fund less leveraged (and thus less risky).

By the beginning of July, the volatility of the fund been reduced by 10 percent.

By July 21, the fund had gained 7.5 percent for the month, but by the end of July the fund had lost all of the gains it had experienced intra month.

August continued the decline across all positions in the fund. On Aug 17, Russia defaulted on its government debt but LTCM had only a small exposure to Russian government debt and the fund suffered a small loss.

On August 21, LTCM had significant interest rate swap trades that performed poorly. There was also a significant loss in merger arbitrage positions related to the planned acquisition of Ciena by Tellabs. Total loss for the day was a staggering $550 million.

On August 21, the fund's capital was now $2.95 billion. The leverage ratio that had been at 28 at the beginning of year now stood at 42. That meant for every dollar of capital, LTCM had $42 worth of positions on its books.

Sunday August 23, the principals of LTCM met in their offices in Greenwich, Conn. They held discussions regarding the lack of market interest in their positions, and what to do about the declining capital base. They had $2 billion of working capital but if the fund continued declining, it would alarm the dealers/banks who lent them credit and result in unfavorable terms. What to do?

The fund chose to reduce the risk of its portfolio and attempt to raise additional capital, but couldn't redeem itself. LTCM continued to struggle and eventually needed the Federal Reserve and a consortium of major Wall Street banks to bail them out of the debt that they were in.

What went wrong? A number of factors contributed to the failure, among them over-zealous confidence in flawed statistical models and returning a significant proportion of its capital base. Why did LTCM return capital to its investors? LTCM felt that its capital base was too big and it was trying to maintain high returns on the reduced capital in the fund. In hindsight, LTCM should not have returned the capital—during the meltdown, it needed more capital to fund the trades that it was forced to exit. LTCM was forced to reduce its leverage exposure and therefore having the additional capital would have reduced the leverage exposure and thus the risk of the portfolio. LTCM also made a major mistake when it liquidated the most liquid positions in its portfolio first.

Liquidity and Illiquidity

Liquidity: Liquidity refers to the degree to which a position can be bought or sold in the market without affecting the position's price. Liquidity is characterized by a high level of trading activity—stocks in the S&P 500 are generally very liquid.

Illiquidity: Something is illiquid when it takes a long time to buy or sell the position in the market without aversely affecting the position's price. A house is generally referred to as an illiquid asset.

LTCM's risk/reward analysis showed the most profitable trades were the most risky ones; unfortunately these were also the most illiquid positions in its portfolio. While LTCM believed that this would be the best way to increase the returns and try to make back the heavy losses, this made the portfolio even more risky.

The Washington Post described the collapse of Long-Term Capital Management as "one of the biggest financial missteps ever to hit Wall Street." *The Wall Street Journal* called the fund "one of [Wall Street's] most aggressive offspring" and the Financial Times described it as "the fund that thought it was too smart to fail." *BusinessWeek* simply wrote that "Long-Term Capital's rocket science exploded on the launch pad."

Amaranth and the Natural Gas Bubble

More recently, Amaranth Advisors LLC became a kind of poster boy for those seeking greater regulation of the hedge fund industry. It all started in 2005 with an energy trader named Brian Hunter. In the wake of Hurricane Katrina, Hunter correctly bet that natural gas prices would go through the roof, and he bought up a number of derivatives to, essentially, bet on that climb. Hunter was right, and natural gas futures surged to all-time highs at the end of 2005.

That's when Hunter guessed that futures would go even higher. He not only bet that they would, but he took on leverage to bolster his returns. At one point, he was levered eight-to-one on his bet.

In a word, he lost.

Natural gas futures slid steadily throughout 2006—by mid-year, they were almost as low as they were at the start of 2005. According to media reports, Hunter kept betting, hoping for a turnaround. A few reports claimed he hid the results of his failed trade in a desk drawer. Ultimately, there was nothing left to bet, and the tab came due. Amaranth had $9 billion under management—and lost $6.5 billion on the natural gas trade, leaving investors like Morgan Stanley and Goldman Sachs holding the bag. The fund was suspended on September 29, 2006, and on October 1, the fund hired Fortress Investment Group to help liquidate its assets.

The losses certainly weren't on the scale of Long Term Capital, but they did help illustrate the need for regulatory compliance and oversight. Amaranth's collapse prompted numerous hedge funds to improve their technology and oversight to prevent such an occurrence. Today, it's highly unlikely that a single trader could hide so much, for so long, and threaten the very existence of a fund.

Major Hedge Funds

A funny thing happened as the hedge fund industry grew in recent years— traditional Wall Street firms took notice. Back in 2003, the list of the top 25 hedge funds was dominated by privately held funds. Today, the top funds, listed by assets under management, come with names like Goldman Sachs, Barclays and Man Financial. Instead of outsourcing their money to hedge funds, these major financial institutions simply created their own, hiring top managers, pouring in their assets and turning them loose. The results are impressive.

In 2003, Caxton Associates was at the top of the list with $10 billion under management. In 2006, that jumped to $12.5 billion, but that was only good enough for 10th place. Goldman Sachs' hedge fund is now on top with a whopping $21 billion under management. That's followed by Bridgewater Associates, with $20.9 billion under management. D.E. Shaw, which is 20 percent owned by Lehman Brothers, is third with $19.9 billion.

Visit the Vault Finance Career Channel at **www.vault.com/finance** — with insider firm profiles, message boards, the Vault Finance Job Board and more.

V/\ULT CAREER LIBRARY

53

Research & Rankings – 2006

Rank 2006	Firm/Fund Name(s)	Capital ($millions)
1	Goldman Sachs Asset Management	21,023
2	Bridgewater Associates	20,886
3	D.E. Shaw Group	19,900
4	Farallon Capital Management	16,400
5	ESL Investments	15,500
6	Barclays Global Investors	14,330
7	Och-Ziff Capital Mgmt Group	14,300
8	Man Investments	12,700
9	Tudor Investment Corp.	12,683
10	Caxton Associates	12,500
11	Citadel Investment Group	12,000
12	Campbell & Co.	11,500
13	Perry Capital	11,325
14	GLG Partners	11,241
15	Cerberus Capital	11,200
16t	Lone Pine Capital	11,000
16t	Maverick Capital	11,000

Rank 2006	Firm/Fund Name(s)	Capital ($millions)
18	Moore Capital Management	10,200
19	Angelo, Gordon & Co.	10,000x
20	Soros Fund Management	9,600
21	Atticus Capital	9,200
22	Brevan Howard Asset Management	8,975
23	HSBC	8,853
24	J.P. Morgan Chase & Co.*	8,826
25	25 HBK Investments	8,812

* Includes Highbridge Capital Management
Source: *Alpha Magazine*

GETTING HIRED

Hedge Fund Job Search Basics

CHAPTER 5

Questions To Ask Yourself

All of us go through a decision-making process when choosing the right career and the right career path. In this section, we take a look at the questions that you might want to ask yourself as you consider pursuing a career in the hedge fund industry. Please note that our answers serve as a general guide and are not reflective of every situation or job type. The majority of your answers will be slowly uncovered by you during your own search and due diligence process.

How much structure do I need?

Like most finance jobs, jobs at hedge funds tend to be analytical, and require you to be highly interactive with a variety of people. However, they do not have the same corporate infrastructures as large investment banks. A lot of individuals who thrive in these jobs are self-starters and very motivated because there aren't necessarily any training programs or standardized job descriptions at hedge funds.

What would be my ideal work environment?

Hedge funds are much smaller (number of total employees) compared to large corporations, especially investment banks. The largest hedge funds will have a few hundred employees; the smallest ones have two employees. Consequently, there is generally less corporate bureaucracy, a less rigid corporate structure, more free flow of ideas and less work politics.

Geographically, where do I want to be located?

Hedge funds are proliferating all over the globe (North America, Europe, and East Asia) and are primarily based in (but not restricted to) large metropolitan areas within major financial hubs such as New York, London and Hong Kong. Recently, there has been growth in the number of hedge funds located in suburban areas around major cities (such as Westchester County or Connecticut). Hedge funds are increasingly locating themselves in these

Visit the Vault Finance Career Channel at www.vault.com/finance — with insider firm profiles, message boards, the Vault Finance Job Board and more.

VAULT CAREER LIBRARY   59

Hedge Fund Job Search Basics

areas because of the lower costs of office space. In general, hedge fund managers have great flexibility in choosing their location—you can run a hedge fund out of anywhere as long as key technology such as telephones, trading platforms, and e-mail are present. Still, locating near a major financial hub is advantageous because it makes it easier to meet with investors and other industry contacts.

What is most important—a high starting salary or financial security?

The hedge fund job starting salaries are generally on par with the rest of the financial industry for entry-level jobs. But depending on the type of position, there is sometimes a larger financial upside at a hedge fund for young, bright individuals, particularly in areas such as trading. A lot of hedge funds will hire smart, young individuals, whose compensation will be directly correlated with the trading profits generated for the fund portfolio. At the same time, there isn't the same guarantee of pay increases as there is in a more structured environment like an investment bank.

It is very important to perform thorough due diligence of a potential hedge fund employer and consider the financial security of the potential position. Hedge funds have varied lives, ranging from two years to 20+ years, which means that if you land with a hedge fund that goes under, you might find yourself looking for another job after two years. Heading into investment banking brings more stability.

How important are quality of life issues?

Hedge fund job hours vary depending on the type and level of the job. Your own research of a specific job will help you answer this question.

How quantitative am I?

The responsibilities of a hedge fund position vary depending on the function. But for most positions, quantitative analysis will play an important role. All hedge fund employees, even those in non-investment decision roles such as operations and investor relations, need to have a certain knack for numbers. Equity-only funds can be a little less quantitiative, as they only deal with stock. Funds that employ more complex security products such as derivatives, convertible bonds, and so on, require even stronger math skills.

How important is long-term job security?

As stated in earlier chapters, the hedge fund industry is growing at rapid rate and, in our opinion, is not going to go away for a long time.

Will a graduate or professional degree help me attain my career goals?

Graduate degrees

Graduate degrees such as the MBA, JD and Ph.D., are required and/or helpful for senior jobs (i.e. credit analyst, research analyst) and also make it easier to get in the door. For junior positions, it is usually not necessary to have an advanced professional degree. Some of the larger hedge funds offer financial aid to help employees get professional degrees if they get their degrees in part-time programs while continuing to work at the fund.

Professional certifications Series 7 and Series 63: For junior trading positions, hedge funds will typically immediately sponsor an employee for the Series 7 and 63 exams. The NASD Series 7 General Securities Representative exam is the main qualification for stockbrokers, and is normally taken in conjunction with the Series 63 Uniform State Law Exam. This qualification can open many doors in the financial services industry.

CFA: The CFA (chartered financial analyst) program has three levels of examinations and measures the candidate's ability to apply the fundamental knowledge of investment principles at the professional level. This is also a useful advanced course, primarily for research analysts and similar positions.

Advice from an MBA

Jason, a newly minted MBA, offers his advice on landing a job in the hedge fund industry.

"As a newly minted MBA, an appropriate strategy to securing a position is two-fold: First, it helps to find a fund with a strategy that overlaps with your professional history. The ability to take sector-specific knowledge (that you gained prior to B-school) and apply it to a fund's investment philosophy or thesis is an instant value-added play for them. Secondly (and kind of on the contrary), expressing that you are comfortable being uncomfortable is key—smaller funds will embrace your industry

Visit the Vault Finance Career Channel at **www.vault.com/finance** — with insider firm profiles, message boards, the Vault Finance Job Board and more.

VAULT CAREER LIBRARY

61

knowledge, but are sometimes looking for a jack-of-all-trades and a master of none—be willing to learn the business from the ground up."

Jeff, 24, recently promoted to associate in a major hedge fund

"I knew at the start of my senior year, back in late 2003, I wanted to get in on hedge funds. I had interned at a major investment bank in New York, but sales and trading on those big desks didn't appeal to me, and there were only so many slots on the M&A teams. I went ahead and applied for a bunch of S&T programs with the big guys through the fall of my senior year, but I also started networking pretty heavily. In the spring, it turned out that one of my supervisors at my internship went to work for a hedge fund. So I got in touch, and he remembered me right off the bat. I managed to get in to see him when I went to New York for my interviews in the spring. When I got there, he had the head of trading with him, and we ended up there for about four hours. In the end, I got one of the first analyst-level jobs they created at the firm. And now they're huge, and I'm an associate. I've learned so much about so many different trades—like what I would've been doing at the I-bank, but on steroids."

Cathy, 31, hedge fund currency/rates strategist

"I hadn't planned on working for a hedge fund when I was in school getting my MBA. I was a broker for years, and decided to get the MBA to broaden my portfolio of skills. I guess I took a shine to currencies, and ended up writing my thesis on carry trades. That got published about six months after I got my degree. I was already back with my old firm then. And the fund called and asked if I wanted to come in. And now I'm signing off on any and all carry trades the traders want to do and suggesting new ways to do it. I think it goes to show that hedge funds are always on the lookout for up-and-coming talent."

Researching Hedge Funds

Once you have decided what role interests you, you need to research the companies and potential job opportunities available. There are many ways you can learn about the industry and opportunities.

Professional organizations

Associations are a useful research tool for the job search. While many professional organizations cater to Wall Street jobs and careers in general, there are specific organizations that focus solely on the hedge fund industry. An extensive list of professional organizations is located in the reference section in the Appendix.

Student organizations

As an undergraduate or graduate student, many schools have student organizations that cater to finance students. Examples include the University Finance Association or the Graduate Finance Association. This is one way to see if there are hedge funds that visit your campus or faculty members with research in this area. You may also want to speak with your alumni center to see how to contact any alumni in the hedge fund industry.

Networking

When you begin your career, try to make contacts with people in the industry by looking for internships with hedge funds or investment banks. Networking at social events or business functions can mean that you get to meet people in the hedge fund industry or who know of people who work in the industry.

Databases

The web sites of hedge fund advisors typically maintain internal use databases of hedge funds and/or publish directories. Most of this information requires a password for access, but some is available for free. An extensive list of databases and hedge fund advisors is located in the reference section at the back of this book.

Industry news

There are a variety of hedge fund newspapers on the Web. An extensive list of the best sites is located in the reference section at the back of this book.

Internships

Formal internships are usually not available at many hedge funds. This is because most hedge funds are smaller offices with no separate human resource department to facilitate an internship program. Still, many undergraduate and business school students looking to break into the industry

Visit the Vault Finance Career Channel at **www.vault.com/finance** — with insider firm profiles, message boards, the Vault Finance Job Board and more.

VAULT CAREER LIBRARY

63

Internship Stories

Phil, a second-year MBA student, realized that his previous experience in investment banking could translate into using those skills in an analyst position with a hedge fund. By networking through alumni from his school, he contacted many different hedge funds. He eventually interviewed with a hedge fund manager and took an unpaid internship just to get into the industry.

Mike is a junior undergrad majoring in finance who is currently interning with a fund of hedge funds. Mike wanted to break into Wall Street and realized that hedge funds were particularly interesting to him. As an intern for 10 hours a week, he gets to watch the analysts and portfolio manager make trading decisions and see first-hand what a hedge fund does. His responsibilities range from developing databases, researching companies to general assistance for the analysts and portfolio manager. The internship is unpaid, but he realizes that the experience he is getting is invaluable.

Philip managed to secure his internship through his school's career center. He is a German student studying for his MBA in finance. His prior experience was working for a large German bank performing analysis of customer loans and various financing transactions. He was able to parlay these skills to admission to a top business school and then learned more about trading and finance. The business school had a student-run fund where the students got hands-on trading experience, which translated well for him at his internship. Although the internship was paid, it was low pay because the hedge fund was small.

Steve worked for a pension fund prior to going back to get his MBA and conducted stock analysis in his previous job. He chose to get an MBA to expand his knowledge in finance and become a better analyst. He used his previous contacts to contact hedge funds in a major city; his contacts recommended him to the funds. He was able to land a notable fund.

From college to a hedge fund

Like any other entity in the financial services industry, hedge funds can, and do, hire people fresh off their undergraduate work. That said, this is somewhat rare. Smaller hedge funds have no need for undergraduates to help run their companies. "When you only have 10 employees, and you're managing $500 million in assets, you can simply go out and hire the best," says one fund co-founder. "Every employee here has at least five years' experience elsewhere, and most have ten. If you don't need to train from the ground up, why should you?"

That's the conundrum facing undergraduates looking to break into hedge funds: experience. Hedge funds, especially smaller ones and ones that are just starting up—which is the vast majority of funds—use their founders' and employees' experience as their main selling point. In a ten-person shop, where the lead managing director spent 20 years, say, managing Merrill Lynch's emerging markets investing, your undergraduate degree will pale in comparison. And if they're doing their jobs right, they can afford to simply steal employees away from larger organizations.

Larger funds, however, provide more opportunities. As mentioned above, you can expect to start small—on a level comparable to an analyst at a major investment bank. You will probably be one of only 6-15 employees at your level of experience, with the rest in far more senior roles. You'll likely be sponsored for your Series 7 and 63 if you're in trading, or be taken under the wing of a more senior employee if you're involved in other aspects of the fund.

Salaries will be comparable to the overall industry—about $50,000 to $75,000 a year, plus bonus, but this can vary widely from fund to fund, as can the bonuses themselves. If you're at a smaller fund that has a good year, the bonus money can be double your salary, but this is rare. Large funds, run like smaller investment banks, will give you $20,000 to $30,000 in bonus money your first year.

From there, you'll have to prove your worth. The more responsibility you can handle, of course, the more money you'll make. There are tales, mostly apocryphal, of undergrad whiz-kids coming into the hedge fund world with the next big idea for trading or minimizing risk, and allegedly making $1 million in a few short years. That's unlikely, so don't get your hopes up. You'll be comfortable financially, but you'll work long hours for it.

Landing that hedge fund job right out of college won't be easy. Most hedge funds refrain from advertising in the newspaper or even on financial job boards. Most work through executive recruiting agencies. Only the largest funds have begun the process of reaching out to the top business schools in their search for up-and-coming talent. You'll be fortunate if one or two show up at your school's career fairs. That means the onus will be on you to find a good match.

Thankfully, if you're a business or economics major, or are at a school with strong programs in these areas, you'll have some resources at hand. College career centers are working hard to reach out to the industry, given the students' interest, and it's a poor business program that doesn't have a number of alumni currently involved with hedge funds. The contacts should be there—it's up to you to work them to your advantage.

Key attributes

What are hedge funds looking for in undergraduate students? Ideally, you'll already have had a strong internship between your junior and senior years, at an investment bank or other top-tier financial company. Your exposure to big-league operations, trading or research will be a major asset. In addition, your undergraduate academic work has to be top-notch, and ideally focused on cutting-edge investments, risk mitigation or portfolio theory. Your concentration in management issues won't do much here! (Which, of course, has led to other apocryphal tales of tyrannical hedge fund managers—thankfully, few are true, despite the intensity of the industry as a whole.)

With a strong internship and excellent academics going for you, it'll still be up to you to get yourself out there. This book lists the top hedge funds in the United States, and is a great launching point for your career search. There will be other, smaller funds in your area, or the area in which you wish to live, that you'll have to research and find. Once you know which funds you want to explore, you'll have to get on the phone, find out who hires, find out their hiring policy and send along resumes and work examples. You may end up sending out fifty resumes to get one or two bites, but given hedge funds' relative reclusion compared to the major investment banks, this is to be expected.

Review and hiring

From there, you may find yourself on telephone interviews, doing written tests, traveling to meet with fund managers—all on a schedule that will likely seem haphazard. While most investment banks and major financial corporations have a very detailed hiring process, a hedge fund with even 100 employees likely hasn't bothered with a formal undergrad hiring process. Indeed, you may have to gently prod your potential employer about the status of your candidacy—but with great discretion, of course.

A handful of funds *do* adhere to the kind of review and hiring schedule that their investment banking forebears created. In that case, you may have already explored the funds through their campus visits. You'll know where to send your materials, and their human resources department will promptly schedule you for a telephone interview, written work, and a spring break interview. If you're interviewing with investment banks or major money-center banks as well, then you'll find the process very similar as well as convenient.

Investment banks

Speaking of investment banks, these massive institutions may be a perfect way for you to enter the hedge fund industry. Most hedge fund founders, managers and employees started in sales and trading, or research, within these major corporations. Indeed, the outsized profits of investment banks in the past two years haven't come from the typical IPO and M&A advising—their proprietary trading desks increasingly adopt the strategies and tactics of hedge funds. You may find the structure of these organizations comforting as you learn the investment trade. They provide valuable, structured experience that you can then parlay into a better-than-entry-level hedge fund job in a few years' time.

You may also want to consider working directly for the alternative investment arms of these major investment banks. You'll note that the list of top hedge funds in this book includes funds under the aegis of Bank of America, Credit Suisse, Goldman Sachs, J.P. Morgan Chase, Lehman Brothers and UBS. Merrill Lynch and Morgan Stanley also have very strong hedge funds working right within the larger company. Some of these firms will work with particularly bright candidates to place them within these internal hedge funds, while others will require a few years' work and advancement to the associate level before offering positions in these units. Either way, they are compelling alternatives to hooking up with a smaller hedge fund, especially if you're concerned about the churn rate smaller hedge funds have seen in recent years.

Visit the Vault Finance Career Channel at **www.vault.com/finance** — with insider firm profiles, message boards, the Vault Finance Job Board and more.

VAULT CAREER LIBRARY

67

Companies like Goldman Sachs, after all, aren't going anywhere any time soon.

Hedge fund opportunities for recent MBA grads

The typical hedge fund has a great deal more interest in newly-minted MBA graduates than undergraduates. Not only are MBA holders far better educated, they also tend to be more specialized, and can fill the niches within a hedge fund more readily, especially when it comes to smaller hedge funds. Combined with a few years' experience in other financial services industries, the new MBA graduate can generally find interest among hedge funds.

Hedge funds have done a better job reaching out to business graduate schools than they have the undergraduate programs. Nearly all major hedge funds boast several MBA graduates from top business schools, and there's a distinct bias toward bringing in new workers from these familiar programs. "I graduated from Wharton, and I know what that means. When I have an opening, I'll give the school a call and see who's coming up," says a fund manager with $2 billion under management. "I know that if I need a specialist in Latin American corporate bonds, somebody there's probably done his thesis on it at some point."

The process for hiring MBA grads is still somewhat informal compared to the detailed processes investment banks use. Yet there's also a stronger alumni outreach effort, and much stronger career placement centers that can help you reach out to many hedge funds with relative ease.

Specialties

There are hedge fund jobs out there for most MBA specialties, from portfolio theorists to hardcore statisticians. Indeed, hedge funds' strategies often hinge on finding the right specialists. One fund may specialize in risk management and arbitrage across a wide variety of asset classes, while another may specialize in intense research and modeling of each individual holding. One of the more unusual examples is Renaissance Technologies, founded by mathematician James Simons, which generally prefers mathematicians with PhDs over MBA holders.

While an unusual example, Renaissance Technologies leads to another good point. Hedge funds tend to be small, so the more a given employee can handle, the better. Degree programs that offer both an MBA as well as an advanced degree in mathematics, economics or actuarial sciences can make a candidate even more compelling—so long as the candidate's academic work has real-world applicability.

Mid-career transitioning to a career in hedge funds

Despite everything we just discussed about post-collegiate hedge fund careers, most people in the industry have transitioned into hedge funds from elsewhere. Indeed, it seems a month hasn't gone by over the last four years where a couple of vice presidents or managing directors from major investment banks have formed their own fund. And you'll find that they often take some of their best underlings with them.

If you're already in the financial services industry, you probably already know someone who's taken the plunge and joined a hedge fund. Experience is in demand, and if you've proven your abilities in a given specialty, you'll likely find transitioning to a hedge fund relatively easy.

That latter point is particularly important. If you've simply been on the trading desk for a few years and haven't really contributed to your company's overall strategy within your specialty, you'll have a harder time finding a hedge fund interested in you. Hedge funds want the best, and they can afford to pay the best. Racking up returns in a fairly easy trading environment—domestic equities from 2003-2006 or emerging markets from the turn of the century to now—doesn't necessarily qualify. You should have contributed meaningfully to your company's success in a given area, innovating and charting a strong course in whatever you do. Developing a strong research metric for determining corporate bond valuation, creating a new risk arbitrage strategy between currencies and equities, even developing a way to evaluate hedge funds when creating a fund of funds—all these are the kinds of things that hedge funds are looking for.

That can sound onerous for the average person, but then, the average person doesn't cut it in hedge funds. Hedge funds represent a frontier within the financial sector, and an entrepreneurial spirit is very much a requirement for most fund employees. It takes a special person to innovate and succeed at an investment bank—and it takes an even more special person to join a hedge fund, no matter the size of the fund, and leave behind the success and the bonuses that an established institution fosters.

Visit the Vault Finance Career Channel at **www.vault.com/finance** — with insider firm profiles, message boards, the Vault Finance Job Board and more.

VAULT CAREER LIBRARY

69

If you feel you've been a success in your industry thus far and want to explore hedge funds, the first thing to do is to talk to former colleagues and associates who have already joined funds. Given the relative newness of the industry and its exponential growth this decade, the trail has only recently been blazed. Your contacts in the industry can lead you to funds that may be interested in your talents.

You may also want to contact the major placement firms that service the financial industry, such as Capital Search Group, RJ Associates or the Lucas Group. Your contacts in the industry can further advise you on the best firm to help place you, given your experience and expertise. Hedge funds often go to such firms to help them discreetly find the employees they need. In what's become an increasingly competitive environment, a blanket job notice from a hedge fund could tip a fund's hand as to future strategy, after all.

"Personally, I think it's time to think about moving to a hedge fund when you start to get feelers coming in," says one investment bank vice president who, she admits, is considering the shift to a hedge fund. "I really hadn't considered it until I got that first call from a friend of a friend who used to work with me." Such a call, she says, let her know that she had a skill set and experience that was in demand. "I didn't take that job, but it got me thinking and starting to put out feelers of my own," she says. Getting that call was her first sign that she could have success in the field.

Of course, you may not want to wait. In that case, the best thing to do is to ensure that your current resume shines. You may even wish to transfer to a different department to fill in a hole in your skill set, or to notch another, more recent success before you start looking. If you feel you have what it takes already, then register with the search firms and start talking to colleagues, rivals and contacts. The hedge fund industry is still relatively small when it comes to hiring, and word-of-mouth goes a long way.

Interview Questions

Interviews at hedge funds vary depending on the type of job that you are applying for. Many job interviews begin with behavioral questions. Through behavioral questions, interviewers seek to learn what type of employee (with regard to attributes such as work ethic, leadership, and teamwork skills) you will be. They are also "fit" questions designed to see whether you pass the the airport test—i.e., can the interviewer stand to be stuck with you at an airport for eight hours?

Behavioral Interview Questions

"Practice makes perfect!" We hear this often, but we sometimes forget to take our own advice. Making time to practice your responses to interview questions is essential to a giving clear, thought out, insightful answer. In a typical 30-minute interview you might be asked anywhere from half a dozen to a dozen questions (often depending on the length of your answers). But what will the questions be?

Below, we take a look at common behavioral interview questions.

The basics

1. Walk me through your resume.

2. Why do you want to work for us?

3. What interests you about our company?

4. What are our strengths?

5. What are our weaknesses?

6. What skills do you bring to the job?

7. Why do you feel you will be successful in this role?

8. What can you do for us that your peers cannot do?

9. What is it about our industry that interests you?

10. What is it about our industry that you find least appealing?

11. Why this job?

12. What qualities do you think are important for this job?

13. What are you looking for in a job?

14. What is the most important part of a job to you?

15. What can you do to increase our sales/productivity/customer base, etc.?

16. Why should we hire you?

Tell me about a time when... Give me an example of...

17. Tell me about a time when you had to rewrite the rules.

18. Give me an example of a time when your boss was wrong in their assessment of a situation, and how you handled it.

19. Tell me about a time when your decision was contrary to the groups' decision.

20. Tell me about a time when you had to identify and obtain the resources necessary to complete a major task.

21. Give me an example of a time when you worked on a team and one member wasn't doing his/her share.

22. Tell me about a time when you faced more work than you or your team could reasonably handle.

23. Give me an example of the most complicated presentation you've ever made; what kind of information were you trying to communicate?

24. Tell me about a time when you were directly involved in a significant disagreement about what needed to be done.

25. Give me an example of a time when you had the opportunity to demonstrate your functional expertise.

26. Give me an example of your analytical thinking skills.

27. Tell me about a time when you had to use your ability to solve problems.

Career and academic decision and outcomes

28. Why did you attend XYZ College for your undergraduate degree?

29. Why did you decide to return to school for your MBA / MPA?

30. Why did you choose XYZ as your concentration?

31. What was your undergrad GPA?

32. What is your grade point so far?

33. What's the best job you've ever had? What made it so good?

34. What's the worst job you've ever had? What made it so bad?

35. What would your dream job be?

36. Tell me about the best work environment you've been in. What made it so good?

37. Tell me about the worst work environment you've been in. What made it so bad?

38. Why did you leave a particular job you previously had?

Insight about you

39. What would your former work colleagues say about you if I called them?

40. Tell me about your greatest strength and biggest weakness.

41. What have you done to correct this weakness?

42. What kind of manager / supervisor / team lead / team member are you?

43. Have you ever found it necessary to break/bend the rules?

44. What is the best decision you ever made?

45. What is the worst decision you ever made?

46. What kinds of decisions are the hardest for you?

47. Imagine we are six months in the future.

48. Who else have you interviewed with?

About starting the job

49. What job would you choose over this one?

50. What kind of salary are you looking for?

51. How much do you think this job is worth?

52. What questions do you have for me about starting the job?

53. When can you start?

Visit the Vault Finance Career Channel at **www.vault.com/finance** — with
insider firm profiles, message boards, the Vault Finance Job Board and more.

V/\ULT CAREER LIBRARY   **73**

Hedge Fund Knowledge Interview Questions

After the behavioral questions, the interviewer is likely to ask more technical questions about the job. This may occur at any point in the interview process (first round or subsequent follow-up interviews).

1. What is a hedge fund?

It's a private, unregistered investment pool encompassing all types of investment funds, companies and private partnerships that can use a variety of investment techniques such as borrowing money through leverage, selling short, derivatives for directional investing and options.

2. Why would you want to work for a hedge fund and not a mutual fund?

This question varies by individual, but think about examples like the following:

You have a specific interest in the fund manager's strategy. You were always interested in merger arbitrage, fixed income arbitrage etc.

You don't like to be confined by the stricter rules that mutual funds have to follow and would appreciate the ability to look for short positions and/or use derivatives.

You would like to work in a smaller shop—many mutual funds are huge—and therefore if you like smaller, possibly more challenging, work environments then state this.

3. What makes hedge funds different?

The main distinguishing characteristics are that hedge funds use derivatives, can short sell and have the ability to use leverage.

4. What is convertible arbitrage?

It's an investment strategy that seeks to exploit pricing inefficiencies between a convertible bond and the underlying stock. Managers will typically long the convertible bond and short the underlying stock.

5. What does it mean when a manager says that he is "event-driven"?

That's an investment strategy seeking to identify and exploit pricing inefficiencies that have been caused by some sort of corporate event, such as a merger, spin-off, distressed situation, or recapitalization.

6. What is the strategy of our fund?

• This is specific to the firm you are interviewing with. Try to do the following:

• Search the Web to find any articles on the fund.

• Search Bloomberg to find any articles written on the fund.

• Use the Hoovers database to see if the management firm is listed.

• Refer to the reference section to see how to find out whether the fund has any information posted in the databases.

Once you have found the strategy that the fund is pursuing, research the current environment of the fund. For example, if it is a merger arbitrage strategy, look to find any recent announcement mergers and be prepared to discuss your opinions on it.

7. What are the key issues that you think our fund must face?

This answer will be specific to the firm you are interviewing with.

8. Give me an example of a sector trade.

Review Chapter 3 to brush up on hedge fund trading strategies. Here's an example of a sector trade: Fred is a long/short equity hedge fund manager whose primary trading strategy focuses on sector trades. Fred noticed that in the tech sector, Microsoft (MSFT) was a relatively cheap stock when compared with Oracle (ORCL). Fred purchases 100 shares of BSC because MSFT is undervalued relative to the theoretical price (fair value) and the market is expected to correct the price. Simultaneously, Fred sells short 100 shares of ORCL because ORCL is overvalued relative to its theoretical price.

	Beg price	Sell price	Profit
Buy 100 shares of MSFT @	30	35	500
Sell short 100 shares of ORCL @	12	10	200
Total			$700

Visit the Vault Finance Career Channel at **www.vault.com/finance** — with insider firm profiles, message boards, the Vault Finance Job Board and more.

VAULT CAREER LIBRARY   **75**

Fred predicted that the price of Microsoft would rise and the price of Oracle would fall. He was correct and made a total profit of $600.

9. What important trends do you see in our industry?

SEC regulation, growth in institutional investing and the potential of offering hedge funds to average retail investors are all key issues.

Operations Questions

After a general overview of hedge funds, the interviewer will likely ask you job-specific questions. These are now broken down by job types that have been discussed in this book. Please note that these are just to be used as a guide and are no means exhaustive. We have highlighted clues for answers to some of the questions but it is best to prepare for these questions with a thorough understanding of the topic and industry.

1. What is meant by "leverage"?

Leverage measures the amount of assets being funded by each investment dollar. The primary source of leverage is from borrowing from financial institutions; an example in everyday terms is a house mortgage. Leverage is essentially borrowing by hedge funds using their assets in the fund as a pledge of collateral toward the loan. The hedge fund manager then uses the loan to buy more securities.

The amount of leverage typically used by the fund is shown as a percentage of the fund. For example, if the fund has $1 million and is borrowing another $2 million to bring the total dollars invested to $3 million, the leverage used is 200 percent.

2. What is a prime broker?

Prime brokers offer hedge fund clients various tools and services such as securities lending, trading platforms, cash management, risk management and settlements for administration of the hedge fund.

3. What role does it play for hedge funds?

A prime broker provides the hedge fund with useful tools for portfolio management.

4. What is meant by margin?

Buying on margin is using money borrowed from a prime broker to purchase securities.

5. What is short selling?

Short selling involves the selling of a security that the seller does not own. Short sellers believe that the stock price will fall (as opposed to when buying long one believes the price will rise) and that they will be able to repurchase the stock at a lower price in the future. Thus, they will profit from selling the stock at a higher price, then buying it in the future at a lower price.

6. Do you know what the difference between a put and a call option is?

A put option gives the holder the right to sell the underlying stock at a specified price (strike price) on or before a given date (exercise date). A call option gives the holder the right to buy the underlying stock at specified price (strike price) on or before a given date (exercise date). The seller of these options is referred to as the writer—many hedge funds will often write options in accordance with their strategies.

7. What is meant by the term "securities lending"?

This is a loan of a security from one broker/dealer to another, who must eventually return the same security as repayment. The loan is often collateralized. Securities lending allows a broker/dealer in possession of a particular security to earn enhanced returns on the security through finance charges.

Accounting Questions

1. What is an offshore administrator?

The offshore fund entity that manages the back office work and individual accounts for the fund.

2. What is the difference between an onshore and an offshore fund?

Onshore structures are normally set up as a limited partnerships. Because of this, tax obligations flow directly through to the partners, and the funds avoid the double taxation that exists for a corporation. There are two components to the limited partnership: the general partner and the limited partners (hedge fund investors). The general partner is an individual or corporation responsible for the management and operation of partnership. This is normally the "hedge fund manager." The limited partners are the investors whose liability is limited to the amount of money they invest into the partnership.

Offshore structures are normally organized outside the U.S., usually in an offshore tax haven—the Cayman Islands, Bermuda, the British Virgin Islands, the Bahamas or Ireland. Typically a corporate structure, but because of the tax haven no entity level taxation is imposed, taxation occurs at the investor level. Instead of a GP, a management company is used. Investors purchase shares. Offshore administrators provide weekly/monthly NAVs that funds distribute to investors.

3. What are the main issues to look for when reconciling the accounts?
Ensuring that the prices of the securities are correct, ensuring that all trades are accounted for. Checking the dividend and interest payments.

4. What is a 10-K?
It's a report similar to the annual report, except that it contains more detailed information about the company's business, finances, and management. It also includes the bylaws of the company, other legal documents, and information about any lawsuits in which the company is involved. All publicly traded companies are required to file a 10-K report each year to the SEC.

In addition to these hedge fund-oriented types of questions, there are likely to be more specific accounting questions relating to CPA issues.

Trading Questions

1. Where do you think interest rates will be one year from now?
You should have your own opinion on this and be prepared to back it up.

2. Who is Alan Greenspan and what does he do?
Alan Greenspan is the chairman of the board of governors of the Federal Reserve System. He took office for a fifth four-year term on June 19, 2004. Dr. Greenspan also serves as chairman of the Federal Open Market Committee, the system's principal monetary policymaking body.

3. What do you think of the economy and interest rates?
You should have your own opinion on this and be prepared to back it up.

4. What does the yield curve currently look like, and what does that mean?
Look up current yield curves and be prepared to explain their potential movements.

5. What happened in the markets during the past three months?
Make sure you stay on top the markets.

6. Do you read The Wall Street Journal everyday? What's on today's front page?
Read *The Wall Street Journal* religiously.

7. Your colleague tells you he's swamped and asks you to look over a credit swap agreement. You agree and tell him it looks fine. He signs off on it and gives it to his manager. Later, you realize that you overlooked a material clause and that it adversely affects the firm. What do you do?
You accepted the responsibility, so you take the fall. Talk to your colleague and then both of you go to the manager.

8. You have to get a swap agreement done by Friday. You fax it to your counterparty and he agrees to get back to you immediately. On Tuesday, you call to determine the status. The person you talk to informs you that the counterparty is on vacation and won't be back for a week (the person on the phone is filling in for your normal contact). You mention the swap and the guy says he'll take care of it. Later that afternoon you receive a fax of the swap agreement with no changes made to it. What do you do?
Relationship management. It's a legally binding agreement, but the agent (new guy) probably doesn't have a clue what he's doing and it's not worth messing up the relationship over this. Call the new guy, explain the situation and have him contact your normal counterparty or have his supervisor to sign off on the deal.

9. Do you invest in stocks personally?
Be prepared to discuss your personal portfolio.

10. What stocks do you like? Why?
This is basically a stock pitch. Be ready to talk about three stocks in detail. Know financial information, ratios, multiples, the company's prospects, etc. HINT: Consider giving the investor relations office (of the stocks you are

Visit the Vault Finance Career Channel at **www.vault.com/finance** — with insider firm profiles, message boards, the Vault Finance Job Board and more.

VAULT CAREER LIBRARY   **79**

pitching) a call as part of your preparation. Asking the company questions shows that you have really done some homework.

11. Tell me about what you consider your best investment success? Biggest failure? What did you learn?

Again, be prepared to discuss your personal investments.

12. Do you have specific industry interests?

If you aren't naturally enthusiastic about markets, you won't thrive at a hedge fund.

Risk Management Questions

1. What is VAR – value at risk?

VAR is a methodology which uses statistical analysis of historical market trends and volatilities to estimate the likelihood that a given portfolio's losses will exceed a certain amount.

2. What does the term delta mean?

It is the change in price of an option for every one point move in the price of the underlying security (a first derivative).

3. What is meant by gamma?

Gamma is a measurement of how fast delta changes, given a unit change in the underlying price (a second derivative).

4. What does the term vega mean?

Vega is the change in the price of an option that results from a 1 percent change in volatility.

5. What is meant by Rho?

Rho is the dollar change in a given option's price that results from a 1 percent change in interest rates.

6. What does the term theta mean?

Theta is the ratio of the change in an option's price to the decrease in its time to expiration, also called time decay.

Investor Relations Questions

1. What type of investors can invest in hedge funds?

Hedge fund investors are traditionally wealthy individuals and family offices, pensions, endowments and institutions. "Accredited investors" and "qualified purchasers" are the two types of investors that can invest in hedge funds. (More detailed explanations are found in the glossary.) Accredited investors are individuals who have a net worth in excess of $1 million or income in excess of $200,000 individually or $300,000 when income is combined with a spouse. Qualified purchasers are entities that both hold and control $25 million in investments and also individuals or families of companies with $5 million in investments. Therefore only wealthy individuals, families and companies with large amount of investments can invest in hedge funds.

2. Can hedge funds market their funds?

No, not in traditional forms. Marketing via traditional means (TV, newspapers, web sites) is prohibited by the SEC since hedge funds are classified as private partnerships. Getting information about a hedge fund is very difficult for the average investor.

2. How do hedge funds market their funds?

Primarily through word-of-mouth and meetings with potential investors.

Interview Reminders

- Indicate that you have a career plan that has always included this job as your end objective.

- Show how decisions and past experiences have positioned you for this job.

- Know what the firm's investment philosophy is (i.e., momentum, top-down growth, bottom-up value, etc.) and be able to talk about it.

- Know the strengths and weaknesses of the firm very well.

- Know the latest news regarding the firm with which you are interviewing.

- Look for any news the firm has been involved in.

- Know their largest holdings (if possible).

Visit the Vault Finance Career Channel at www.vault.com/finance — with
insider firm profiles, message boards, the Vault Finance Job Board and more.

VAULT CAREER LIBRARY

81

Other Kinds of Questions

Do you feel the hedge fund industry is properly regulated?

This is a tough question designed to put you on the spot. Regulation of the hedge-fund industry remains a hot-button issue, and hedge funds feel very strongly about the positions they've taken.

To properly answer this question, you need to understand the current regulatory framework in which the industry operates, as well as the various proposals out there to alter that framework. The Securities and Exchange Commission's Web site, http://www.sec.gov, is a good place to start, as is a strong archive of news stories on the topic. The *Wall Street Journal* Online, http://www.wsj.com, has extensive coverage of this issue, and a search through Lexis-Nexis, http://www.lexis.com, will give you an even more thorough grasp.

Once you understand the issue, you'll likely have formed an opinion on it. Now you'll have to square that opinion with that of your potential employer. Most major hedge funds have written the SEC on the topic, and their comment letters are likely in the SEC database, again available online. Some hedge funds haven't bothered, however, so you'll be stuck giving your opinion without really knowing what your potential employer thinks.

The vast majority of funds, like most businesses, believe less regulation is more, and increasing the regulatory requirements for funds will eat into their profits. That, of course, is the short answer. You'll need to get more in-depth, however, to really make an impression. If you're interviewing for an S&T job, know about data archiving requirements and trade clearing. If you want to be a trader, know the latest proposals on funds' freedom to trade. If you want to get into marketing, especially, know the details of the SEC's current regulation on sales to qualified customers.

Finally, we come to the answer to the question. Give your opinion, be honest, and show that you've come to it logically, rather than giving a "me too" answer. If there are minor areas in which your opinion diverges from the status quo or the firm's public stance, be ready to defend your answer. If you're talked into a corner, admit that your interviewer has given you some things to consider going forward—but don't cave after five minutes of debate! Hedge funds want logical thinkers and committed personalities, not yes men.

Of course, if your idea of proper regulation of the industry is markedly different from that of the firm to which you're applying, you may want to reconsider working there!

If you put in your time and do well, you stand to make a lot of money working here. What do you think you'll do with it?

This tricky question serves a number of purposes. It tells the interviewer about not only your character, but also your investment philosophy, your future career plans and your potential loyalty to the fund.

As you're likely very well aware, hedge fund managers put a lot of their money into the funds they run. Certainly, saying you'll pour your rewards back into the fund is likely the preferred answer, but should only be a starting point. This is also an opportunity to discuss your hobbies and beliefs. If you donate time or money to charity, this is a good time to mention that, if you plan on supporting your causes with any new wealth. Helping your family is always a good answer as well. You can also discuss a bit about the lifestyle you hope to lead, but here you may not want to go overboard. Nobody goes into this industry with miserly intent, but keeping your materialistic ambitions modest is probably a good idea.

In the end, be honest, but with an eye toward promoting yourself as a competent individual and team player. Nobody's expecting you to be a saint, but a laundry list of the hottest cars, watches and vacation homes is too much at this juncture. Helping your brother through college, supporting Habitat for Humanity and perhaps picking up that Midtown apartment you've been eyeing is a good example—with excess rolled into the hedge fund, of course!

As a concluding part to the interview be prepared to ask questions about the company. Be sure to conclude the interview with an expression of interest in the job. After the interview, follow up with thank-you notes and e-mails and be aware that there may be follow-up exams that you will be required to take. Good luck!

Visit the Vault Finance Career Channel at **www.vault.com/finance** — with
insider firm profiles, message boards, the Vault Finance Job Board and more.

VAULT CAREER LIBRARY   **83**

ON THE JOB

Overview of Hedge Fund Departments

CHAPTER 7

Organizational Structure of a Typical Hedge Fund

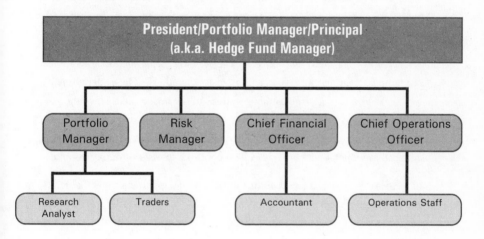

So what exactly are hedge fund managers and what do they do? A hedge fund manager is normally the founder and the key person in charge of overseeing the whole operation of the hedge fund. This would mean that he/she would be responsible for overseeing the portfolio, often making trading decisions, hiring personnel, monitoring the risk of the portfolio and ensuring that the accounting and operations departments are in order. The hedge fund manager is often referred to as the principal or president and can also be called the portfolio manager.

Hedge funds vary in size of assets under management from as little as $1 million to over $10 billion. Compared to roles in the investment banking industry, the roles of hedge fund professionals differ more widely, depending on the specific hedge fund. An entry-level trader at an investment bank is likely to have a role very similar to a trader at another investment bank. In contrast, traders at hedge funds are likely to have different responsibilities depending on the firm. These difrerences are usually determined by the size of the fund. At a smaller fund, the trader is much more likely to be involved with the operations of the trade, whereas a larger hedge fund would have a

Overview of Hedge Fund Departments

separate operations person to handle this element. A smaller hedge fund may have three to four employees, whereas a larger hedge fund may employ more than 300 people.

A typical hedge fund will have the following departments: operations, accounting, trading, and risk and investor relations. These departments support the trading decisions and operations of the hedge fund. Since the size of hedge funds varies dramatically, the number of people in each department can range from one to over 20. As a hedge fund grows in size (manages more money), more personnel are added to support the increased trading volume.

In the next few pages we will outline the different departments at hedge funds and the distinct roles within each department. Note that specific job titles are not formalized from hedge fund to hedge fund. A particular job (function) can have many different titles depending on the hedge fund. For example, an operations analyst at one fund might be called a portfolio analyst at another, or a trading assistant or accountant at other funds.

Because of the varying sizes of hedge funds, employees often have a more diverse range of responsibilities than professionals at investment banks or mutual funds. These responsibilities may straddle several different departments. The versatility demanded of these hedge fund positions requires superior teamwork skills and the ability to deal with a variety of people.

Hedge Fund Culture

Because hedge funds vary widely in size, it is difficult to generalize about the the culture of hedge funds. Many small hedge funds are run like small businesses where the culture of the firm is determined by the owner, or in this case, the hedge fund manager. A fund's strategy also often is a major influence on the culture of the firm. For example, a statistical arbitrage fund is likely to be staffed with Ph.D.s who are less outgoing and enjoy crunching numbers at their terminals. By contrast, a global macro fund is more likely to have a more outgoing atmosphere with the employees watching the markets from a trading floor and more openly sharing ideas. These are two stereotypes of the cultures of different trading strategies and are not applicable to all statistical arbitrage and global macro funds, but the

stereotypes still give you an idea about the types of cultural differences you can expect.

Working at a hedge fund is not like working at an investment bank or a traditional mutual fund. Investment banks and mutual funds are generally large organizations that include support departments that ease the workload of the investment bankers or traders at a mutual fund. For example, there are human resource departments that manage the recruitment of new employees and marketing departments who oversee the marketing of the firms' services to investors and clients. Most hedge funds do not have large human resource or marketing departments—these responsibilities are instead taken up by the managers of the funds. This also means that employees end up pitching in to help in areas that they normally aren't involved in at I-banks or mutual funds, such as interviewing potential new employees and helping to put together marketing materials.

Because they have a lot at stake with the success of their funds, hedge fund managers are (on the whole) more intense than traditional mutual fund money managers. They are more likely to be involved with the day-to-day running of the firm, which means that the manager will have a higher level of involvement and interaction with most of the staff than at I-banks or mutual funds. Still, as a hedge fund grows, this interaction is inevitably reduced somewhat as the manager hires and delegates some of the operational and trading responsibility to new employees.

On the whole, the culture of a hedge fund is less structured and more likely to wear business casual than an investment bank or mutual fund. Also, the whole firm is usually focused on the success and performance of the fund, which tends to make for a cohesive and collaborative working environment.

Visit the Vault Finance Career Channel at **www.vault.com/finance** — with
insider firm profiles, message boards, the Vault Finance Job Board and more.

VAULT CAREER LIBRARY   89

A Day in the Life: Chief Investment Officer at a small, growing hedge fund

6:00 a.m.: The car picks me up at my place in Connecticut. I've been up just long enough to shower and get ready. The driver's already got my papers for me, and we swing by Starbucks before getting on the road. I usually spring for his coffee too. I spend the time in the car reading up on the news and getting on the BlackBerry to catch up on e-mail.

7:30 a.m.: I'm at the office, depending on traffic. My secretary gives me a fresh copy of the previous day's trades, our current positions and any overnight changes in currencies or foreign markets that may have changed our picture. I finish writing up my daily note that I started the night before.

9:00 a.m.: The daily note is done and sent. I grab another cup of coffee before heading to the morning meeting.

9:30 a.m.: Here the management team puts our heads together on our current positions and any pending moves. New ideas come up, as do new areas of concern. Nothing really huge today, so after the meeting, the head of research and I get together for a few minutes to divvy up assignments.

10:10 a.m.: On the way back to my office I go through the trading floor and talk with the guys on the desks there. If there's something unusual happening, I'll make a note to investigate further.

10:30 a.m.: I meet with my strategists and go over our holdings, step by step, like we do every day. Most of these are "no change," or "nothing exciting," but there's generally something every day that bears analysis. Why is Japan off 2 percent today? Domestic discretionary isn't being hit as hard as we thought. Those kind of things. We have theses and theories for every market we're in, and we constantly challenge them—when the market isn't challenging them for us.

11:30 a.m.: I hop on an earnings call for one of the companies we've shorted. Their earnings this morning were a little better than we thought they'd be. The researcher who first found the position is with me on the call. We talk about whether the company still has the vulnerabilities we thought it did. After the call and some number crunching, it turns out that they do. They got lucky this quarter. I drop an e-mail to the management team, recommending we boost the position.

1:00 p.m.: I run out the door for lunch. Today we're meeting with representatives of a private endowment that's interested in placing a big chunk of their money with us. They already have the PowerPoint and the data on the fund. This is the personal touch that'll allow the fund chairman to close the deal. And after two hours, that's exactly what happens.

3:30 p.m.: Back in the office, going over the European results for the day and getting a preliminary feed on the day's trading. I start composing tomorrow's daily note, with the short recommendation front and center.

4:30 p.m.: I start getting the data on the day's trading. The vast majority of our positions saw gains. I get out onto the floor again, chatting with the traders informally. Then it's back to the desk.

5:30 p.m.: We have a quick conference call among the management team, just a few minutes, to talk about any big changes. It was a positive, quiet day, nothing too exciting. I then wrap up the domestic part of my daily note, leaving the international portion until the morning.

6:00 p.m.: The gym. I need it.

6:45 p.m.: The car picks me up. Thanks to easy traffic, I'm back home by eight for dinner with some friends.

11:30 p.m.: Dinner's over, and I spent about a half-hour on the computer checking on a few things overseas. Nothing exciting, so I head to bed for my six hours of sleep. I usually try for seven, but dinner threw me off.

Visit the Vault Finance Career Channel at **www.vault.com/finance** — with
insider firm profiles, message boards, the Vault Finance Job Board and more.

VAULT CAREER LIBRARY   91

Portfolio Management

Like many areas in the hedge fund industry, the term "portfolio manager" can be rather vague and may refer to a number of different roles within the hedge fund. Each hedge fund uses different terms for their managers of specific strategies and for the principals who run the fund. In an effort to simplify the use of the term, the next section defines the term "portfolio manager" into the two most frequently used terms: referring to a person running a particular strategy within a larger hedge fund and to a person managing the entire hedge fund.

Portfolio managers must have advanced knowledge of the financial markets. Portfolio managers utilize a variety of complex and interesting trading strategies. In addition to having a good hedge fund strategy, the portfolio manager must also have:

• Extensive experience and knowledge of portfolio management

• Knowledge on tax implications of trading decisions

• Knowledge of risk management for the strategy and portfolio

• Asset allocation experience

• Generating performance statistics

• The ability to give compelling client presentations for capital raising efforts

Leading a Specific Fund Strategy

Some portfolio managers lead a specific hedge fund strategy with a large hedge fund that utilizes multiple strategies. Before assuming this responsibility, these portfolio managers need to be proven in research, stock selection and portfolio management with the capability of directing research and trading. This position requires at least 5 to 10 years experience in the specific strategy, an MBA (and often a CFA) and a proven performance record, experience managing portfolios, strength in the strategy research (usually fundamental research and valuation) among other requirements.

For example, a portfolio manager could be leading a strategy concerning health care equities as part of a larger long/short equity hedge fund. The portfolio manager would not only be part of the analysis effort, but would

Portfolio Management

also manage the traders and research analysts that also cover the strategy. (In this case, the traders and research professionals would research and trade health care stocks.) This position normally reports to the overall hedge fund manager, discussed next.

Managing the Overall Hedge Fund

The portfolio manager who runs the overall business is often the founder of the hedge fund. This person is likely to have a minimum of 10 years of investment experience and has gained experience as an excellent stock picker or has generated consistent positive returns on a trading desk. In order to establish and run his own hedge fund successfully, the individual needs to:

• Understand the financial markets and investment theory completely

• Come up with the trading and investment strategy for the portfolio

• Develop a marketing and capital raising business plan

• Work closely with attorneys and administrators to set up the hedge fund

• Recruit, select, hire and retain skilled, trusted and experienced employees to oversee different aspects of the fund

Portfolio managers who run the entire fund must have the ability to run a small business and deal with human capital issues. At larger funds, this portfolio manager has the chief operating officer, chief financial officer, head of trading, head of risk and head of research report as direct reports. At smaller funds, the portfolio manager is often responsible for all the research and trading himself, and also manages the operations and administrative staff.

Stepping Stones to Portfolio Management

How do recent MBA grads become portfolio managers? The answer is to build experience with a proven track record of analyzing and trading a specific strategy, which can be done as a research analyst at a buy-side firm or at a smaller hedge fund. In order to become a portfolio manager who runs one strategy at a larger hedge fund, the key is to have portfolio management experience, research experience and a proven track record.

As a principal of a fund, the person needs to have extensive industry contacts (in order to raise capital), an extensive and proven track record and the ability to manage a small business.

Compensation and Individual Investment

The main difference between portfolio managers at hedge funds and portfolio managers at mutual funds is their compensation structure and the opportunity for individual investment in their firms. These key differences are explained in depth in the following sections.

Compensation structure

Portfolio managers (as principals of the firm) are compensated in two ways, with a performance fee and a management fee.

- General management fees. These typically range from 1 to 2 percent of assets under management. Management fees support the general upkeep of the hedge fund office; electricity, office space, trading technology and salaries.

- Performance fees. These are generally 20 to 25 percent of the fund's returns (performance) over a given period and are designed to align manager interests with their investors.

- Both the performance and management fees are paid for by the investors from their assets in the fund, to provide incentives for the analysts, traders and risk managers. Portfolio managers usually share the performance fee with their staff in the form of year-end bonuses

Individual investment

The majority of portfolio managers invest a significant proportion of their own capital within their own fund. High personal investment aligns manager interests with those of their shareholders. Most potential investors look for whether the portfolio managers have invested in their own fund and what proportion of net worth the portfolio manager has invested in the fund.

Our Survey Says: Portfolio Management

High manager investment levels signal to investors that the portfolio manager believes in his strategy since he is willing to invest a significant proportion of their capital in the fund.

Getting in: "Paying your dues"

Eric, portfolio manager/principal — start-up hedge fund

"I put my time in on Wall Street before I got to this stage. Right after I graduated from Harvard Business School, I started working for CIBC on their proprietary trading desk. I traded on the same desk for 10 years without one down year the whole time. Then I went over to Lehman and ran their institutional equity trading desk for four years and expanded their client base by three fold. Through knowledge, research and luck I have somehow always picked the right stocks. Now I am running my own show, and although there is a lot of pressure to perform well and raise capital for the fund, I don't have to deal with all the politics at a large investment bank. To any young graduate considering eventually becoming a portfolio manager I recommend getting an early start in research and/or trading. These are the most valuable areas needed to eventually start your own hedge fund. Lots of hard work and focus will get you there."

A Day in the Life: Portfolio Manager (Principal) at a medium sized hedge fund

8:30 a.m.: Have driver of the Mercedes town car drop me off in front of the office, while he parks the car in the garage in the basement of the office building.

8:45 a.m.: Arrive at the office and ask the secretary for messages and a rundown of meetings and appointments for the day. Skim through The Wall Street Journal and Financial Times and look for any latest news on the stocks in the portfolio. Scan the sectors the fund invests in. No alarming news.

9.00 a.m.: Stop by the research analyst desks to discuss any breaking news for the portfolio and then head over to talk to the head trader on what happened in after hours trading yesterday and how the stocks fared. Discuss the trading plan for the day and advise covering as much of the ABC short position as possible, even if the stock is not liquid in the market.

9:30 a.m.: Look over the printout from the accounting group on the security level performance in the portfolio. Evaluate trends, and see if any stock lost more than 1 percent. Have the research team investigate these further.

9:45 a.m.: Attend the scheduled meeting with two senior individuals in the risk management group who want to pitch in buying the latest risk software for $20,000. Listen to the pros and cons of the software, take notes and determine what added value this software will have to the firm. Let the risk staff know that you will get back to them with a decision after conducting some more research. Risk management also gives a briefing during the daily morning research meeting—brief overview of all upcoming conferences, meetings, and so on, and gives a general guidance of the stocks to focus for the day.

11:00 a.m.: Call in the secretary and have her go on the Internet and print a list of all risk software available in the market and their prices.

11:15 a.m.: Conference call with legal counsel on recent SEC changes on shorting stocks and get their opinion on how this may impact the firm.

12:00 p.m.: Lunch with an investor in town from London. He just wants to touch base on how things are going on at the fund.

2:00 p.m.: Come back from lunch and check on how the portfolio is doing relative to the market. Speak with the head of trading and get a recap of the trading day so far.

3:00 p.m.: Meet with the investor relations department to check the status of the presentation being prepared for tomorrow's important meeting with a large institutional investor who is considering investing a large sum of money into the fund. Ask for a draft and review for any changes.

4:00 p.m.: Market close. Check news for any aftermarket close news releases.

4:30 p.m.: Get the intra-day P&L to see how the fund performed for the day.

5:00 p.m.: Discuss the conference call highlights with the legal counsel on the changes in SEC short rules with the traders and the CFO and have them implement any relevant changes.

6:00 p.m.: Attend hedge fund managers conference at an investment bank that is one of the fund's prime brokers.

7:30 p.m.: Network with fellow industry professionals at the cocktail hour reception of the conference.

9.00 p.m.: Leave the event and go home.

Research

The typical research department at a hedge fund is composed of research analysts and associates who are responsible for company valuation, sector analysis and forecasting the effect of events on the market and the economy.

Research analysts work in conjunction with quantitative analysts and portfolio managers to research and evaluate stocks using financial models that take into account sales, costs, expenses, depreciation and tax rates (among other data points) in order to determine the value of a company and project future earnings.

Research Associate/Analysts

Research professionals at hedge funds must process and analyze information at lightning speed and work independently without too much guidance. People who do well in this position generally have a passion for the markets and dogged perseverance when ferreting out information that could affect stocks.

• Research analysts at a hedge fund have the following responsibilities:

• Assisting portfolio managers and traders

• Conducting extensive research on the companies assigned to them

• Maintaining databases of historical and current financial statements of the firms they cover

• Running financial models and performing valuation analysis on companies, using sources that include:

• Research reports written by staff at investment banks

• Public announcements

• Data gleaned from conferences and trade shows

• Conversations with management at the company in quest

• Interviewing the company's clients and competitors to ask them what they think of the company

• Assessing current trends in business practices, products, and industry competition

• Keeping abreast of new regulations or policies that may affect the industry

• Monitoring the economy to determine its effect on earnings

Research analysts use spreadsheet and statistical software packages to analyze financial data, spot trends, and develop forecasts. After they have drawn their conclusions, they write reports and make presentations, usually making recommendations to buy or sell a particular investment or security. Senior analysts may actually make the decision to buy or sell for the company or client if they are the ones responsible for managing the assets.

In order to extract the information needed to evaluate stocks, research analysts interact with industry professionals and senior level officials at companies under evaluation, conducting interviews and attending conferences. Research department positions require exceptional quantitative skills, people and time management skills and the ability to process and decipher large amounts of information.

At hedge funds, the difference between research associates and research analysts is not as distinct and clear-cut as it is at an investment bank. At investment banks, associates typically put in several years of time and hard work before they are given a chance to perform complex research as an analyst. At hedge funds, they do more complex research work earlier in their careers.

Research Fundamentals

When researching a company, research analysts look at a company's growth (profit) prospects and how undervalued or overvalued the company's price is relative to its prospects. There are several methods of fundamental research, which are described below.

Top down

This method involves looking the market as a whole and predicting which sectors will perform better than others. The research analyst then recommends companies in the sector of choice. The focus here is picking a good sector rather then picking a good company.

Top down example: Rebecca analyzes the sectors that constitute the S&P 500 Index. She narrows down to three sectors (financial, entertainment and health care) that she thinks will perform well. Rebecca further analyzes each of these sectors and finally recommends several stocks within the financial sector to buy.

Bottom up

Using this method, a research analyst chooses companies that match the portfolio's risk and ratios criteria and within this "basket" analysis a few names, selecting those that will presumably perform well.

Bottom up example: Jen is a quantitative analyst at a leading hedge fund and has built a model that has several variables it will look for. She uses a basket of 500 names in this model that will generate about 10 to 20 names that match the criteria of each variable. Quantitative analysts then work with the research analysts to find the best names to purchase or short.

Value of a company

In this type of research, a research analyst looks at the financial balance sheets (income, inventory, expenses, debt, cash flows, etc.) of a company along with its risk premium in order to find the best stocks to buy or short. All stocks deemed to be undervalued are bought and ones that are overvalued are shorted.

Using the DuPont Model

The DuPont ROE analysis uses the most recent financial statements available. With the DuPont analysis, the analysts would also run the financial statements of industry comparables (getting this data either from proprietary models and databases or from Bloomberg), to get the industry DuPont analysis. The analyst then assesses the health of the company using the DuPont factors—what is the company doing well and/or poorly compared with its competitors? The analyst then writes a report and that is presented to the investment committee, which usually consists of the portfolio manager and other analysts.

Value of a company example: Fred is a research analyst at a small hedge fund. He reviews the accounting statements of a large Fortune 500 Company and uses the DuPont Model to calculate its ratios and those of its competitors. Fred finds that the firm he covers has a higher sales ratio and lower expenses than its competitors, but its price to earnings

Visit the Vault Finance Career Channel at **www.vault.com/finance** — with insider firm profiles, message boards, the Vault Finance Job Board and more.

VAULT CAREER LIBRARY   **101**

> ratio is lower. After further investigation, with proprietary evaluation metrics, Fred decides that the company is undervalued relative to its peers and issues a buy recommendation.

Career Path and Compensation

A common career path for recent undergrads and MBA graduates looking to get into hedge fund research is to work as an analyst or associate at a major Wall Street bank, gain specific experience in a specific sector, build relationships with hedge funds (who could be clients) and then transition over to a hedge fund. For example, a prospective research analyst could work in the health care, defense or technology industry and parlay this experience to being an analyst in the hedge fund industry. MBA students at top programs should also be on the lookout for large hedge funds that come to recruit at the very best schools. These positions are rarely available through recruiting agencies.

The junior research analyst role involves grueling hours (upwards of 80 hours a week during earnings season) and lot of perseverance. Beginning research analyst positions pay between $100,000 to $150,000 depending on past experience and education background.

At larger hedge funds, successful analysts can move up to a senior research analyst level, where they have several research professionals reporting to them. Ultimately, successful research professionals can become portfolio managers. If they don't ascend to this position at the firms they are working for, many research analysts branch off to start their own hedge funds. Senior research positions pay from a few hundred thousand dollars to well into seven figures, depending on the size of the firm and its pay structure.

A Day in the Life: Research Analyst, Large Hedge Fund

6:30 a.m.: Arrive at the office, finish reading the article in the Financial Times on Company ABC's recent investigation by the SEC.

7:00 a.m.: Check e-mails and news on Bloomberg and CNBC to see if there are any earnings announcements or other news that might have an effect on the companies being covered. Print all research reports sent daily by analysts at investment banks.

7:30 a.m.: Attend daily morning research meeting with the senior analysts who give a brief overview of all upcoming conferences and meetings and discuss stocks of particular interest that day.

8:00 a.m.: Call industry contact covering stock ABC to get a better scoop on what is going on with the SEC investigation since the fund owns 100,000 shares of ABC and it was recommended by the senior analyst as a stock that was very undervalued.

8:30 a.m.: Type notes from earlier call in an e-mail and send details to the senior analysts. Review the daily P&L distributed by the accounting group and categorize securities by sector in a spreadsheet that you maintain daily.

9:00 a.m.: Sit down with the portfolio manager and review ideas in the pipeline. Discuss securities that did not move in the anticipated direction.

10:00 a.m.: Attend two sessions of a biotech conference held by an investment bank. This gives you the opportunity to meet management directly in companies XYZ and BCD. You question them about future plans for the company as well as trends in the biotech sector.

3:00 p.m.: Check the news for any aftermarket news releases.

4:30 p.m.: Update financial models with the closing day's prices and other pertinent ratios to evaluate how the fund performed on the day.

5:00 p.m.: Discuss today's conference highlights with the rest of the research team and try to generate ideas based on the talks.

6:30 p.m.: Conference call with a senior analyst and somebody working on the M&A of companies FGH and JKL to evaluate how the stocks will be priced once the acquisition of JKL by FGH is complete.

7:30 p.m.: Try to work on writing an article for the quarterly newsletter, since the end of the second quarter is coming up.

8:00 p.m.: Go home to order take out and go to bed. The day will start all over again tomorrow.

Our Survey Says: Research

To help you get a sense of life as a hedge fund professionals, Vault brings you the inside scoop via insiders in the industry.

Challenge: "I almost feel like a detective"

Adam—research analyst, medium to large hedge fund

"I guess my title is a research analyst, my business card does not say that, but nobody's business card at my firm has a specific title. I came here after working on the sell-side in the research role for six years. I was covering a lot of the companies that the fund had in their portfolio at the time. The best part of my job is that I am always challenged and no day is the same, so I am never bored. I have to look at the big picture while trying to use the 'small print' as I call it, the things that are not so obvious, to see which company is overvalued or undervalued. I almost feel like a detective. I enjoy working with numbers and statistics, which is a very large part of what I do. There is a lot of pressure and constant deadlines and you are always working on multiple projects at the same time. I have to really prioritize and learn to manage time wisely, otherwise I could get lost in my office.

Operations

The operations department at a hedge fund supports the trading and accounting groups by ensuring that all trades are accounted for and settled correctly. Professionals in operations reconcile the trading positions (of securities) with what the banks know to be correct. If there are any errors, it is the operations department's responsibility to ensure that these get corrected. The operations group often generates daily performance reports for analysts and portfolio managers.

An entry-level professional in this department generally starts as an operations associate. Higher positions on this career path include the director of operations, controller, CFO or ultimately chief operating officer. Many operations staff members also move on to areas such as trading and portfolio management. The "back office'"environment of the operations department is not as demanding as the "front office," but the job is very fast paced and the front office heavily relies on this team for accurate portfolio information.

Front office: The term "front office" is used at a hedge fund and at investment banks to refer the departments that directly produce revenues for the firm, such as sales and trading.

Back office: The term "back office" is typically used to describe departments that support the front office staff (i.e., traders) in trade settlements and other administration.

Operations Associate

This position, also sometimes called "operations specialist" requires a bachelor's degree (one from a top 20 school in finance is preferable). If the employee is not already registered (Series 7 and 63), most hedge funds will sponsor and pay for the employee's licensing within the first six months on the job.

When looking for junior operations personnel, all hedge funds look for young, bright individuals who are willing to put in a couple years doing the grunt work for an opportunity to move up within that area or into a front office role such as trading.

Typical job duties of this position include, but are not limited to, settlements of trades, daily portfolio reconciliation between in-house systems and prime brokers/banks, and phone interactions with brokers.

These responsibilities can be quite time-sensitive. The most time-sensitive issues are related to trade settlement, which involves the actual payment of money to the seller and delivery of securities to the buyer after the trade is verbally agreed upon. Depending on the security and country it is listed in, securities have different standard settlement periods. For example, stocks in the U.S. settle three days after trade date (also referred to as T+3), while options in U.S. settle T+1 (the day after the trade is agreed upon). If a particular trade does not settle, it is considered a "failing" trade. Failing trades require immediate attention as they could potentially cause large errors for the trading desk.

Trade Settlement Example

Here's an example of the trade settlement process:

Day 1 (Trade Date)
Bob, the trader at a hedge fund buys 1,000 shares of IBM at $100 from a broker, Best Executers. Bob inputs the trade in their in-house portfolio management system, which the operations team monitors closely.

Day 2 (T + 1)
The day after the trade date, Cynthia from the operations group notices that she has not received a "confirm" (this can be electronic through the DTC system or a verification from the broker that he has indeed executed the trade) from Best Executers and decides to call Bob to make sure this trade was executed. Bob states that he definitely knows that he got a fill for the trade and will call his contact at Best Executers to make sure there are no problems.

Day 3 (T + 2)
Two days after trade date, Cynthia notices that the trade is still not confirmed with the counter party (Best Executers) and asks Bob for a contact there so she can make sure the trade is OK. During the day she gets caught up in a project and forgets to call Best Executers.

Day 4 (T + 3)
Now, it is the third day after trade date (settlement date) and the price of IBM has gone up to $105. Cynthia finally calls Best Executers and they explain that they "do not know" this trade (which means they do

not acknowledge the trade). Cynthia then conferences in Bob; Best Executors repeats their standing.

Bob calls his contact, who explains that it was his mistake—he never gave the instructions to his operations staff. The trade does not settle on settlement date, but finally on T+4, Best Executers instructs on the trade and it settles.

In a scenario like this, the hedge fund had a trade in its portfolio that it was tracking for P&L (profit and loss). It was also making further trades off the position on IBM stock it assumed it held. If Best Executers had claimed that they definitely did not know the trade, the fund would have to remove the trade from the portfolio, causing the IBM position to have incorrect P&L and quantity for the previous three days. This in turn would have caused incorrect performance reporting. It is especially important that major trade corrections are made before the end of the month, because that is typically when investors are tracking performance numbers.

Operations associates generally report to a senior portfolio analyst or director of operations. Salaries range from $40,000 up to $60,000 plus a discretionary performance-based bonus, which can be 10 to 50 percent of annual salary.

These jobs are typically available through headhunters or job listings. Hedge funds are increasingly utilizing specialized job agencies as a lot of times they don't have time to do the due diligence on each candidate. This way, they get a selected pool of candidates that they can interview. There tends to be high turnover in this position because most individuals in this entry-level position can get bored if their learning curve has diminished and they want to move up within the firm or look for a senior position at a competitor. The job described above with similar responsibilities can also be called trading assistant or analyst.

Career path

Entry-level operations associates work closely with trading and accounting departments, enabling them to learn about different security products, portfolio management, settlements, etc. This broad knowledge base allows them to sometimes move to different roles within the firm such as trading, research or accounting. An individual can also stay in the same function for several years (three to seven). After gaining a wealth of experience, an

Visit the Vault Finance Career Channel at **www.vault.com/finance** — with insider firm profiles, message boards, the Vault Finance Job Board and more.

VAULT CAREER LIBRARY   107

operations associate may have the opportunity to move up to a more senior role with some supervisory responsibilities. If an individual decides to stay in the same role at the same place for several years, he/she will receive salary increases and larger bonuses depending on performance. If the individual's performance has been exceptional, it is not rare to make total compensation (salary and bonus) of $100K-$160K. Ultimately, if someone stays in the role he/she can run the entire operations area as director of operations. The final stage of the career would most likely be chief operating officer (COO), which is usually attained after several years of managerial experience.

A Day in the Life: Hedge Funds Operations Associate

7:00 a.m.: Arrive at the office and log on to the computer and all the various other back-office/portfolio systems. Get coffee and breakfast.

8:15 a.m.: Check e-mails and voicemail and decipher if anything is of urgent matter and needs to be addressed immediately.

9:00 a.m.: Go over all reports of cash and trading activity and trades settlement. Highlight all items that have a potential discrepancy.

10:00 a.m.: Work with the operations team and manager to speak with various departments internally such as trading, risk etc and externally

(i.e. prime brokers, offshore administrators, accountants) in an attempt to resolve any trade errors.

11:00 a.m.: Conference call with UBS Euroclear settlements dept (executing broker) and the prime broker. This call is necessary because a French security trade was booked by the prime broker to settle in the local French market, although the executing broker (UBS) knew to settle via Euroclear. The call is to make sure all involved parties agreed which way to settle the trade. (Euroclear is one of the world's largest settlement systems for domestic and international securities transactions, covering bonds, equities and other investments; see the Glossary for more information.)

12:00 p.m.: Go to lunch with a fellow colleague at a local deli. Lunch varies from a one-hour lunch outside the office on a slow day to a quick sandwich at the desk on a busy day.

1:00 p.m.: The afternoon is generally a combination of phone calls and e-mails resolving all discrepancies from the morning reports.

2:00 p.m.: Work on a project for the principal of the hedge fund. The project involves creating a spreadsheet to show all the brokers who were used for equity trading in the last six months and how much commission was allocated to them.

3:00 p.m.: Make sure all positions and cash activity are accurately reflected in the prime broker reports. Prime brokers of hedge funds provide portfolio and margin level reports daily, which help the funds reconcile positions and cash to their own in-house systems.

4:00 p.m.: Re-review all reports from the morning and make sure all highlighted discrepancies are resolved; otherwise jot them down as "open items."

5:00 p.m.: Address any remaining e-mails that are not time sensitive and look over tomorrow's schedule/agenda.

5:30 p.m.: Recap with manager any items that need his attention.

6:00 p.m.: Leave work and go to the gym facility in the building offered by the job.

7:00 p.m.: Meet friends for some cocktails at a bar and have dinner with them or go home and order cheap Chinese as the job isn't pouring in all the money you would like.

Our Survey Says: Operations

To help you get a sense of life as a hedge fund professional, Vault brings you the inside scoop via insiders in the industry.

Variety: "No two days are the same"

Hillary, 27 – "I have been working at the fund since I graduated college with a history major. I really did not want to go to graduate school and did not know where I would get a job with a history background. My older brother's friend was a trader at the fund so he decided to submit my resume. They were hesitant to hire me because I did not have any finance background, although the timing worked in my favor because the fund was looking for a very junior operations person to support the trading group. Initially all I was doing was inputting trades into the portfolio system, updating spreadsheets and printing and faxing things. I felt like a glorified secretary, although I learned quickly and now I am responsible for all operations of the funds risk arbitrage book. The fund

Visit the Vault Finance Career Channel at **www.vault.com/finance** — with insider firm profiles, message boards, the Vault Finance Job Board and more.

VAULT CAREER LIBRARY   **109**

employs several strategies and there is one designated operations person for each strategy...I really enjoy the variety of different things I cover, no two days are really the same. I am considering getting my MBA after putting in one or two more years in here and then coming back to work in a different role at a hedge fund."

Salary: "My friends are making more than I am"

Jerry, 25 — "I have been at the fund for three years now. First time I came here was for an internship my junior year at NYU while I was studying finance. I really enjoyed the internship because I liked the guys I was working with and learned a lot at the job. I was thrilled when they offered me a job as a portfolio analyst after I graduated. I am still in the same role. I work alongside the traders to make sure all books and records are accurately maintained. I interact a lot with our prime brokers to make sure our trades are settling properly and all their reports match ours. It bothers me that three years have gone by and I am making a lot less money than my friends who are in trading, investment banking, etc. There are many times I am working on weekends and on average I am here 'till 8:00 p.m. every night, whereas my buddy who is a trader is out at 4:30, half an hour after the market closes every day. He works for a large investment bank and gets a percentage of profits he generates. Some months he is bringing home 10 times what I bring home. I know I could do what he does, but now I have this experience in this job. I am not certain what my next step is, but I certainly find my experience here to be invaluable."

Director of Operations

Most individuals carrying this title either have several years of experience in the same capacity, an MBA or both. At this stage one generally has a staff of two to 10 people who are direct reports. The job functions are similar to the operations associate, although there is much more responsibility for the employees working under you as well as maintaining relationships between prime broker, banks, and off shore administrators.

This position will generally pay between $100,000 and $250,000 depending on experience, background and size of hedge fund.

A Day in the Life: Director of Operations

7:30 a.m.: Arrive at the office and log on to the computer, along with various back office and portfolio systems such as DTC. (See Glossary.)

8:15 a.m.: Go over exception reports (available only to a manager) that show trades that have not settled and any Margin Calls for accounts and speak to the member of staff who works on it to get status on the item.

9:00 a.m.: Have weekly team meeting and go over team workload and coverage for the week.

10:00 a.m.: Get on a call with a manager in the prime broker because a large wire needs to be sent out for management fees and there needs to be extra attention given to it to make sure it goes through properly. (The prime broker is described in detail in Chapter 13. It is a department at an investment bank that offers products, technology and clearing services to a hedge fund.)

11:00 a.m.: Have a meeting with the head trader on the convertible trading desk who does not agree with the final position on a particular security. Go over each transaction and see if anything was incorrectly booked. Have one of the staff members print all transaction reports internally and at the prime broker to find a solution to this problem as it may involve large losses for the desk.

1:00 p.m.: Have lunch at the desk while browsing through some stories on Bloomberg.

2:00 p.m.: Field calls and help the staff resolve any pending problems.

4:00 p.m.: Review all reports from the morning and make sure all highlighted discrepancies are resolved, otherwise jot them down as "open items."

5:00 p.m.: Create a list of agenda items for the next day and look at the calendar for any meetings.

6:00 p.m.: Leave work and meet the prime broker, who is taking the operations team out for dinner.

7:00 p.m.: Discuss rates with the prime broker over dinner and get to know her better.

10:00 p.m.: Head home and try to get the motivation to go to the gym before crashing.

Visit the Vault Finance Career Channel at **www.vault.com/finance** — with insider firm profiles, message boards, the Vault Finance Job Board and more.

VAULT CAREER LIBRARY   **111**

Accounting

The accounting department works with the operations group to ensure that the investors' capital and share of profits are accounted for correctly. This means that the accountants reconcile the hedge fund's internal reports with a third-party accountant (usually an offshore administrator) to ensure that their figures are correct.

This department is a crucial part of the hedge fund structure and can serve multiple functions, depending on the size of the firm. At larger firms, the operations and accounting departments are separate and distinct. At smaller firms, the two departments may be combined or the accounting work may be outsourced to a third-party firm.

Accountant

An accountant position generally requires a CPA (certified public accountant) or past accounting experience for even a junior role.

What is the CPA?

CPAs are licensed accountants. To obtain a CPA, applicants must take and pass a two-day, four-part exam. It is not necessary to pass all four parts at the same time; if you pass only two parts you get partial credit and you have to take the exam again to get rest of the credit.

Many large hedge funds look for experience from the Big 4 accounting firms when hiring accounting staff. "Big 4" is the term used in the accounting field to describe the four largest global accounting firms. These are Deloitte & Touche, Ernst & Young, KPMG, and Pricewaterhouse Coopers.

The general duties of an accountant include reviewing broker statements, preparing financial statements, managing portfolio allocations, calculating NAVs (net asset value), keeping track of payments, portfolio positions and transfer of capital or income for clients. At a small hedge fund, the "accountant" may also have to reconcile trades and oversee the trade settlement process.

Visit the Vault Finance Career Channel at **www.vault.com/finance** — with insider firm profiles, message boards, the Vault Finance Job Board and more. **VAULT** CAREER LIBRARY **113**

This position is generally demanding and fast paced. Attention to detail is crucial and small mistakes can mean huge losses for the fund. The salary can range from $45,000 to $60,000 depending on location of the fund, prior experience, college degree and licensing.

Career path

An accounting role requires an undergraduate degree in accounting and/or a CPA certification. Because of these prerequisites, the individuals in this function generally do not move between different departments/roles—they have committed some time building their qualifications in this specific area. A lot of accountants stay as accountants for several years, but can move around between hedge funds or the Big 4 accounting firms.

Accountants can become controllers after a few years of experience. The controller position generally pays in the range of $85K to $140K and can lead to chief financial officer (CFO) position. Many individuals in junior roles can also go to graduate programs such as the MBA after a few years of the job, which allows them to be even more marketable to potential employers.

A Day in the Life: Hedge Fund Accountant

8:00 a.m.: Arrive at work, get some coffee from Starbucks and read the headlines in The Wall Street Journal on the Internet.

9:00 a.m.: Check e-mails and voicemail and decipher if there are any urgent matters that need to be addressed. Prepare for the daily 9:30 meeting with the CFO and other two members of the accounting team.

9:30 a.m.: Meeting with CFO. Discuss open items and implementing new policies and procedures to follow when auditors come to the office.

11:00 a.m.: Check daily activity and statements for any potential audit issues such as the lack of a valid audit trail. Also make sure all daily general ledge entries are accurate.

12:00 p.m.: Usually lunch is ordered and eaten at the desk while working. If an hour is lost during the day eating lunch, that means an extra hour will be spent at night catching up on work.

1:00 p.m.: Conference call with the prime brokerage unit regarding discrepancies on the option charges for the month. Go over the data and ask them to amend these charges.

2:00 p.m.: Work closely with the offshore administrator to compile all accurate tax documentation for the quarterly and annual tax filings with IRS. (Offshore administrators refer to offshore entities based in the Cayman Islands, Bermuda, etc. Their functions are to service investors, offer administrative and operational support, and provide financial tax and compliance reporting, which may include audits and tax documents.)

3:00 p.m.: Attend an afternoon conference sponsored by the prime broker regarding new dividend tax implications on certain types of securities.

6:00 p.m.: Come back to the office and go through the many e-mails that came in while out of the office for a few hours. Respond to most e-mails, tagging some to respond to later.

6:30 p.m.: Write down all open items for the next day and create a spreadsheet of positions with open tax lots for the CFO to review.

8:00 p.m.: Head home and go to the gym to unwind from a hectic day.

Our Survey Says

To help you get a sense of life as a hedge fund professional, Vault brings you the inside scoop via insiders in the industry.

Long hours: "I work at least two weekends out of the month"

Sabrina, 33 – "I was recently hired as a controller at a hedge fund that manages close to $1 billion. I have 10 plus years of experience behind me, initially working at Ernst & Young as an accountant, and a several years as a controller on the fixed income arbitrage desk at Lehman. My responsibilities at this job are similar to the job on the fixed income desk

- reviewing daily P&Ls, assisting in reconciliation of the offshore funds NAV (net asset value), although now I have a lot more responsibility as there are not many employees or support staff at the firm. I directly report to the COO. I tend to be in the office at least 12 hours every day. In addition, during month end, I am generally also working weekends

Visit the Vault Finance Career Channel at **www.vault.com/finance** — with insider firm profiles, message boards, the Vault Finance Job Board and more.

VAULT CAREER LIBRARY   **115**

trying to meet deadlines to have all the accounting work ready and the performance numbers properly calculated. Month-end can be definitely be overwhelming. "

High demand: "I was approached by many headhunters..."

Keith, 23—"My senior year at an Ivy League university I registered in our career center's database to look for jobs in accounting. I did not realize that I would get so much response; I had many headhunters and several prestigious accounting firms calling me for potential job opportunities as a junior accountant. I actually took one of the offers and worked at a large accounting firm for about nine months. One of my clients was a hedge fund, and I was the junior guy working on their year-end audits. After a lot of contact with the CFO, one day he mentioned a job opening and I immediately showed interest. Now I have been at the fund for a year and I am learning a lot. I know the accounting job will always be in high demand."

CFO

An accounting role can lead to a supervisory position and ultimately to a chief financial officer role. The supervisory and CFO positions are well paid, and salaries range from $100K to $300K and up. These roles have significant responsibility and daily functions involve preparing complex portfolio valuations/financial statements; maintaining the underlying accounting records for international funds; liaising with fund managers, brokers and custodians; preparing and maintaining standard operating procedures; approving timesheets; scheduling and monitoring workloads; and supervising a team of accountants. The career path in this field is very rewarding, but is not fast-paced like that of a trader. It usually takes many years of experience to move all the way up the career ladder from junior accountant to CFO.

Big Fund vs. Small Fund

There is a vast difference in the job responsibilities for an accountant at a large fund when compared to a small fund. Two professionals we spoke to provide insight into this difference.

Lisa, a CPA who has been out of school for three years, works for a hedge fund with assets under management of over $1 billion. She says that during the months of December and January she works very long hours to help her boss (the CFO) close year-end books. She also says that everything has to be correctly documented and there is no room for error; it gets very stressful this time of the year. The workload comes and goes but there are definitely a few late night shifts during end of quarters and year-end.

Ken, another CPA, works for a small fund. He indicates that he is not even doing any accounting or audit work. "We have outsourced to a large and reputable accounting firm to make sure we are maintaining proper accounting standards. I work more closely with the trading team, helping them reconcile portfolios, apply proper tax lots and making sure P&L is correct. I like what I do because I am learning a large variety of things."

Visit the Vault Finance Career Channel at **www.vault.com/finance** — with
insider firm profiles, message boards, the Vault Finance Job Board and more.

VAULT CAREER LIBRARY   117

Trading

The trading room is a fast-paced and dynamic environment. A trader at a hedge fund is responsible for buying and selling securities at the best possible price. They are the ones actually executing trades.

Depending on the structure of the specific hedge fund, a trader may or may not also be responsible for the investment decision (stock/bond picking) process. At hedge funds relying on fundamental research, for example, the trader does not make the investment decision. At these firms, research analysts and portfolio managers find the best securities to buy, sell or hedge. And in the case of a statistical arbitrage fund, a computer model will generate large lists of stocks to buy or sell. In these cases, the trader is responsible for making sure the trades generated by research analysts or computer models are accurately executed.

The trader also works to build relationships with brokers on "the J street" (Wall Street). Having strong relationships with brokers is important, as it partly determines how much commission the trader ends up paying for an execution, and even can determine access to shares for an IPO (initial public offering).

Junior Trader

This is an entry-level job that requires the Series 7 and 63 (described earlier; also see the Glossary). In this role, the junior trader helps traders or the head trader with recording trades, making sure the positions in the portfolio are accurate, monitoring daily P&L, and working with the back office staff to ensure all trades are settling with the executing brokers accurately. The position requires a thorough understanding of the securities products (equities, bonds, options), especially the securities that the specific desk trades.

Junior traders typically make between $50K to $70K and can also earn commission. Commission structures vary from hedge fund to hedge fund. As a junior level, you might make 1 percent to 2 percent of what the head trader makes, depending on your level of responsibility and the hedge fund operation. Some hedge funds hire young traders solely based on commissions. Under this scenario, you are likely to get 5 percent to 10 percent of the all the profits you generate for the hedge fund.

Hedge fund trading positions are highly competitive. Generally, you need a math or finance background with a degree from a top five school, but even with those credentials, landing a job is no piece of cake. Large hedge funds occasionally recruit at top tier universities, but usually you have to be knowledgeable about the firms, approach them directly, and maybe even know someone at the hedge fund who can get your resume in the door. An MBA is preferred for trading positions. At many firms, entry-level traders can not advance without an MBA; some may attend business school while working at this position.

While hedge fund jobs are increasingly being listed on recruiting agency web sites, trading jobs are still not heavily advertised. The best way to find opportunities is through networking. One common way to develop contacts is to work on the sell-side (investment banks, brokerage houses or any other firm that provides products and services to hedge funds, which are referred to as the buy-side). From the sell-side you can get exposure to many different funds and build relationships with key trading contacts.

A Day in the Life: Junior Trader at a Hedge Fund

7:00 a.m.: Arrive at work.

7:30 a.m.: After logging on to the computer and checking e-mail, you listen to a few earnings calls for companies that the portfolio manager is interested in trading. Take notes so you can report them back to the traders.

8:00 a.m.: Grab breakfast and bring it to the table while looking at each portfolio the trader covers to make sure positions are reconciled properly.

8:45 a.m.: Work in conjunction with back office and respective prime brokers to ensure all trade breaks resolved.

9:00 a.m.: Start looking at the market on the trading screen (i.e. Bloomberg) and attempt to predict how the stock/bond market will open by analyzing global markets (e.g., Nikkei in Tokyo and FTSE in London) and also S&P Futures index, which trades overnight on the Globex system.

9:15 a.m.: Help the head trader analyze opportunities in the marketplace.

9:30 a.m.: Markets open. Head trader will ask you to call several brokers and get bids/asks for stocks and/or bonds.

10:00 a.m.: Help head trader execute orders by calling brokers or via electronic platform. If shorting securities, then you have to call the prime broker to secure borrows.

12:00 p.m.: Observe what has occurred in the marketplace in the morning: are you facing an up market, a down market? This will allow you to help the head trader come up with possible trading scenarios for later in the afternoon.

1:00 p.m.: Pizza gets delivered for you; the head trader goes out for lunch with portfolio managers/principals. The head trader may sometimes call you from his cell phone and ask you to execute orders.

3:00 p.m.: Begin consolidating all tickets for the day done through various brokers and electronic trading platforms.

4:00 p.m.: Start inputting all trades in the front-end order entry system.

4:30 p.m.: Upload trades to each respective prime broker and make sure all position and P&Ls are accurately reflected. Leave the office for the day.

5:00 p.m.: Go to the gym, usually in the building, and then go home.

Career path

The junior trading job is a great training ground to understand the business. Not all junior traders move up to be a full-fledged trader—there is a lot of competition for that position. Individuals who do not advance from junior trader to trader can either stay in the same role for many years or use their skill set to move into operations or research. Even without an official title promotion, compensation continues to increase every year depending on performance.

To succeed as a hedge fund trader, not only do you need superior math/analytical skills, but also a very distinct set of personality traits. Most successful desk traders tend to be very outspoken and sociable and don't have a problem with a loud, fast-paced atmosphere.

Generally, full-fledged trading positions are hard to attain without a prior track record of generating trading profits. Many hedge funds hire traders from investment banks or other hedge funds because they already have a prior track record.

Traders can eventually attain the role of a portfolio manager. In this position, they are not only responsible for executing the trades, but also the investment decisions. This role is very senior at the hedge fund and typically conducted by the principal or founder of the hedge fund. It generally pays a percentage of commissions on the profits or performance. This is one of the highest paying jobs at a hedge fund, and generally pays seven-figure salaries.

Head Trader

To become a head trader, you need to have a proven track record of generating trading profits and several years of relevant experience. If a hedge fund is looking to hire in this capacity, it will generally hire someone who has been a trader for several years at a brokerage house or another hedge fund. A junior trader may also be promoted to this position. A head trader's compensation, similar to a junior trader mentioned earlier, can be salary plus bonus or commission based. Commission ranges from 5 percent to 10 percent of all profits generated, depending on the hedge fund. The compensation is a direct correlation of the profits made for the firm. This position can pay high six to seven figures.

As mentioned earlier, the responsibilities could include making direct investment decisions or working closely with the portfolio managers and research analysts in making these decisions.

Our Survey Says: Trading

To help you get a sense of life as a hedge fund professional, Vault brings you the inside scoop via insiders in the industry.

Stress: Some days are tough

Seth, 29 – "I have been working in the business for a little over four years and some days are better than others. On days when we are making money, things are great, but when we are down it is the worst feeling ever. A couple days ago we had on a large short USD long EUR position and the dollar finally rallied a bit and we lost $250,000 in about five minutes. My boss, the principal of the fund, got very upset and questioned my decisions. Those days are tough."

Atmosphere: Fast-paced

Liza, 32 – "I have worked as a trader ever since I graduated from business school. I have been working at this fund for about two years, trading mainly OTC (over the counter) stocks. I don't do any of the stock picking; our researchers and portfolio managers just give me a spreadsheet of names they think will be profitable to buy, sell or short. There are different traders for each product, but still the group is small, only about six of us. I am the only woman. Almost all trading floors I have worked at I have been one of the only females. The atmosphere is great. Very fast paced, phones are ringing all the time, everybody is yelling across the room. Some days it gets too male testosterone-oriented, although I have learned to tolerate it. I really enjoy going to work every day."

Visit the Vault Finance Career Channel at **www.vault.com/finance** — with
insider firm profiles, message boards, the Vault Finance Job Board and more.

VAULT CAREER LIBRARY   **123**

Decrease your T/NJ Ratio
(Time to New Job)

Use the Internet's most targeted job search tools for finance professionals.

Vault Finance Job Board

The most comprehensive and convenient job board for finance professionals. Target your search by area of finance, function, and experience level, and find the job openings that you want. No surfing required.

VaultMatch Resume Database

Vault takes match-making to the next level: post your resume and customize your search by area of finance, experience and more. We'll match job listings with your interests and criteria and e-mail them directly to your inbox.

> **VAULT**
> > the most trusted name in career information™

Risk Management

Risk management is not always a distinct department at hedge funds. At small hedge funds, the principals or the trading group will monitor the risk; there are no specific risk personnel. Also, many hedge funds outsource their risk controls to third-party vendors that specialize in providing this service to corporations, hedge funds, mutual funds and other firms. And many investment banks also provide risk management as a value-added service through their prime broker departments (described in Chapter 11).

But at large funds, there is usually a group with the sole responsibility of monitoring and reducing risk. The risk management department proactively monitors each hedge fund, using either propriety or vendor-purchased tools and methodologies for risk management. Based on their analysis, risk professionals implement strategies to either remove or reduce the risk.

Funds of funds are known to have very large risk teams for two reasons: 1) by nature, funds of funds deal with a large variety of securities and 2) the risk group plays a large role in alleviating concerns of existing and potential investors.

Risk Associate

Risk associates play a supporting role in the risk department. A thorough understanding of a variety of trading products (i.e., options, fixed income, mortgage backed securities, swaptions), options risks (i.e., delta, gamma, Vega, rho, and theta; see sidebar later in the chapter) and strong analytical skills are required. The daily job duties include, but are not limited to, maintaining value at risk (VAR) data, back-testing and stress-testing securities within a portfolio and reporting the analyzed data to senior risk management.

Risk professionals also sometimes interact with clients (investors). Larger hedge funds have a designated investor relations employee whose sole responsibility is to field calls from investors, but at smaller funds, investors may call the risk group directly to state and address any risk concerns. A strong risk monitoring system is important to investors, as it reduces the likelihood of error and losses. Investors thus are keen on speaking with the risk team to alleviate their concerns. As discussed, many investment banks offer risk capabilities through their prime brokerage departments. At a prime broker, a risk associate will perform the same duties as at a hedge fund, except he will be monitoring risk for several hedge funds that are prime broker clients.

The risk associate position requires a minimum of a bachelor's degree and a few years of relevant experience. This position pays from $50K to $70K depending on geographic location, previous experience, education skills and size of the corporation.

Risk jobs are found through job agencies or through connections. Generally traders also are well aware of job openings in the risk groups and can be a good source of contacts.

To better understand the job responsibilities in a risk management department, consider Heather, who works in risk management at a hedge fund. Her hedge fund subscribes/utilizes a risk monitoring system designed by a large investment bank. Every morning she performs analysis on the short portfolio measuring how minor changes in the stock market, such as the Dow Jones Industrial Average decreasing substantially in one day, would affect the value of the portfolio. Heather does not have to compute everything manually because the risk system has built-in mathematical models. However, she needs to be able understand what the output of results mean and to be able to verbally communicate this clearly to the traders and portfolio mangers. She utilizes various spreadsheets and graphs to back up her analysis.

Key Terminology for Risk Management

Delta—Change in price of an option for every one point move in the price of the underlying security (a first derivative).

Gamma—A measurement of how fast delta changes, given a unit change in the underlying price (a second derivative).

Vega—The change in the price of an option that results from a 1 percent change in volatility.

Rho—The dollar change in a given option price that results from 1 percent change in interest rates.

Theta—The ratio of the change in an options price to the decrease in its time to expiration, also called time decay.

A Day in the Life: Risk Associate at a Large Hedge Fund

7:30 a.m.: Get into the office and check e-mail. Chat with colleagues about interesting stories in the WSJ.

8:00 a.m.: Daily risk conference call with traders, portfolio manager and principals.

9:30 a.m.: Monitoring the portfolios on one screen while looking at the markets affecting the various securities on another screen. Quantify illiquid positions and valuations risk and compare margin requirements of all positions with the custodian/prime broker making sure you are in agreement.

10:00 a.m.: Call the prime broker risk department and discuss risks involved in utilizing more leverage for a particular option arbitrage fund. Write up a report based on the call to present to the principals.

11:00 a.m.: Compile statistics for the ongoing exception report for non-investment risk issues such as trade settlement, a particular trader leaving the organization, etc.

12:00 p.m.: Checking positions to make sure that the portfolio is maintained within established risk parameters.

1:00 p.m.: Eat lunch at the desk while preparing for the 1:30 meeting with potential investors of the hedge fund who want to discuss business and corporate structure of the hedge fund and its links to the investment manager.

1:30 p.m.—2:30 p.m.: Meeting with investors in a conference room. Emphasize the safety of assets to the investor because of proper risk monitoring.

2:30 p.m.: Recap the meeting with principals, see how it went and make a list of items to follow up with the investor. It is very important that the risk manager gets rid of any potential investor concerns of sudden losses.

4:00 p.m.: Work with the CFO or accounting team to have them clarify a problem you noticed on last month's audit.

5:00 p.m.: Field calls and answer e-mails on all risk and portfolio inquiries to internal and external people.

7:00 p.m.: Look over notes from today and jot down any items that need to be addressed tomorrow.

7:15 p.m.: Review schedule for next day.

> **7:30 p.m—8:00 p.m.:** Head home and get to bed early for a good night's sleep.

Our Survey Says: Risk Management

To help you get a sense of life as a hedge fund professional, Vault brings you the inside scoop via insiders in the industry.

Analytical: Complex material

Christian, 26 – "I work with a risk group at a fund of funds which consists of three senior and two junior people. Our fund of funds focuses on choosing low-risk managers who utilize minimum leverage. We allow our managers to use no more than Reg T leverage and only 20 percent shorts in any given portfolio. We stay away from shorts because they can have unlimited risk. I work with my manager in performing risk due diligence for potential managers. This involves looking at their portfolio with a microscope, making sure leverage levels are appropriate; there are no high-risk securities in the portfolio (i.e. security of a company that is filing for bankruptcy, or a restricted security that cannot be priced, etc). We also have to perform stress-testing on the portfolio to figure out how much market fluctuation a particular portfolio can withhold without causing any large losses, and do other fundamental tests to check historical and potential future risk issues. I am always very stressed about my job because my manager gives me short deadlines for projects. Usually if the partners really get interested in a hedge fund manager because they had a great track record of good returns, they start imposing pressure on the risk team to make sure all is 'kosher' on our end. I am slowly getting used to this environment as I have only been doing this for eight months. Prior to that I was working at a mutual fund doing statistical analysis, which was much more laid-back."

Career path

An individual in the risk associate role will generally stay in the risk area because of the skill sets and experience acquired in the field, although risk professionals sometimes move into the trading area as these two areas work very closely together.

A risk associate can either move to different hedge funds and investment banks or stay at one place and move up to be a risk manager. The risk manager position requires 10 or more years of experience—an individual in a junior risk role will have to be patient and be ready to put in time before receiving a substantial promotion. This senior position generally works closely with the principal of the fund.

Risk Manager

A senior member of the risk department has many years of relevant work experience and/or higher education. Most risk groups will not consider a candidate for a senior position right after receiving an MBA unless he/she has previous experience in a similar field. This position can be stress-inducing as it involves the large responsibility of monitoring potential risk for the hedge fund portfolio.

The risk manager has to ensure that his staff is appropriately trained and qualified, create and apply the correct risk assessment techniques and principles, respond quickly to critical issues, drawing accurate conclusions, and have good interpersonal skills for communication with clients (investors or hedge funds depending on the job). Other high-level responsibilities include investigating exceptions in non-investment risks such as trading errors and writing up analysis of the funds asset/liability risk by examining asset books, liquidity of assets, and means of leverage utilized and redemption terms of investor capital.

The risk manager is a very senior position at a hedge fund or prime broker and can lead to a partnership in a hedge fund. At an investment bank this position will deal with senior staff, including the CEO. The job can be very high paying, ranging from a few hundred thousand dollars to a few million. These senior positions are generally hard to come by due to very little turnover, although starting out at a junior level, paying your dues and being promoted to a senior level is well worthwhile, especially if you enjoy this type of work.

Careers in risk can be very lucrative, challenging, rewarding and stressful all at the same time.

Investor Relations

An investor relations specialist handles relationships with existing investors while marketing to prospective investors. As discussed in the Scoop section, investors in hedge funds range from high-net-worth individuals to large institutions and pension and endowment funds. As is the case with a lot of hedge fund jobs, this role is not a separate function, but is instead filled by a principal or another senior individual at small hedge funds. But as a fund grows, this role becomes more crucial because there can be dozens of investors whose requests for information need to be addressed, and the fund will eventually hire a professional to handle this function full-time.

Some of the job responsibilities of the investor relations professional include writing quarterly and annual performance updates to investors, fielding investor calls and addressing their questions in a timely manner, reviewing pertinent hedge fund documents such as the offering memorandum and subscription docs, helping senior staff perform due diligence on potential investors to ensure eligibility and compliance with anti-money laundering requirements, processing all investor-related transactions such as subscriptions and capital call distributions, and creating PowerPoint presentation materials for the marketing efforts to potential investors.

More and more opportunities for investor relations are becoming available as the type and number of investors in hedge funds continues to grow; job openings can be found on job boards and on hedge fund industry web sites.

Investor relations positions require a bachelor's degree in finance or accounting, a thorough knowledge of a hedge fund and a few years of marketing or customer relations experience. In addition, superior written and oral communication skills are a must.

Because any investor relations position at a hedge fund requires some related experience coming in the door and is not an entry-lvel job, the starting salary is usually higher than entry-level operations or trading positions at hedge funds, ranging from $75K to $125K with a discretionary bonus at year-end.

A Day in the Life: Hedge Funds Investor Relations

7:00 a.m.: Arrive at the office, read The Wall Street Journal on the way into work to brief on current events in the market. Read industry magazines/journals to find out the latest news.

8:00 a.m.: After having coffee and bagel, check e-mails and phone messages from clients. Respond to client's questions concerning performance of the fund and general market conditions.

9:00 a.m.: Work on writing the monthly newsletter. This involves getting all the analytics of the fund, which are obtained from the operations manager. It also requires the fund manager to summarize market conditions for the month and indicate which of the firms' securities were impacted and which were not. You assist the fund manager in gathering the market data.

10:00 a.m.: Get called into a meeting with a potential investor by the hedge fund manager. Present the terms and conditions of investing with the fund—lockup periods, minimum investment, etc. The manager has already gone over the returns of the fund and his investment philosophy.

11:30 a.m.: Leave for a lunch in Midtown with an existing investor in the fund. This lunch was arranged to discuss a potential investment in a new fund that we are launching. Over lunch, you discuss the existing performance of our fund, general market conditions and what differences the new fund would mean to his portfolio.

2:00 p.m.: Arrive back from lunch to many e-mails and voice messages. Respond to the e-mails, and continue to write the monthly newsletter, researching the macro economic conditions for the past month.

3:00 p.m.: Speak to capital introductions group at a leading prime broker to discuss their next conference and to see if the firm can present at it. The conference is full for speakers, but the firm will attend.

4:00 p.m.: Arrange meetings with potential investors for the fund manager. Continue with the monthly newsletter—this usually takes a few full days to complete since the coordination of the different departments can be time-consuming.

5:30 p.m.: Leave for a dinner in Midtown with a potential investor in the fund and the hedge fund manager to discuss the investor's potential investment into a new fund the firm is launching. Over dinner, you discuss the existing performance of our funds, general market conditions and what investing in the new fund would mean to his portfolio.

8:00 p.m.: After dinner, grab a cab home and crash.

Career path

Jobs in investor relations require strong marketing and client service skills. They also require a very strong understanding of hedge funds, particularly the one you are working for. Because you will be marketing the fund to potential investors, you need to be able to explain the fund's strategy and operations in detail.

Investor relations professionals tend to stay loyal to one hedge fund for many years. Salary and bonuses increase with tenure; occasionally (but not often), investor relations professonals are also compensated with commissions or a percentage of all assets brought in for the hedge fund to manage. A senior marketer who has several years of experience and a successful track record can make anywhere from $100,000 to $500,000.

Our Survey Says: Investor Relations

To help you get a sense of life as a hedge fund professional, Vault brings you the inside scoop via insiders in the industry.

People skills are paramount

Lisa – "People skills are the most important aspect of my job. I communicate with large investors and senior individuals day in and day out. Even if I am having a bad day I can't let that reflect on my job. It is especially hard when we are having a string of bad performance months. The investors start getting worried and start calling all the time. For example, one high-net-worth investor, who had a substantial amount of his retirement savings invested in our convertible arbitrage fund that was not doing well, called one day and said he wanted to pull the money out. Then he calls back and said he doesn't. Then he calls again and says he does.

We also do our reporting to investors on a quarterly basis, so the end of each quarter is crunch time—I am in the office late, meeting deadlines.

Visit the Vault Finance Career Channel at **www.vault.com/finance** — with insider firm profiles, message boards, the Vault Finance Job Board and more.

VAULT CAREER LIBRARY   **133**

It is my responsibility to make sure all newsletters go out to each investor, so I work with various departments gathering all the information, presenting it in a proper format and making sure they are mailed out in a timely fashion. Other than during these crunch times, I usually work 8:00 a.m. to 7:00 p.m.; it's not too bad. Overall, I really like what I do because of the different things I learn. One day I am talking to an investor about their risk sensitivity and another day I am learning why a particular strategy at our fund had bad performance. It is a demanding job, but I never get bored."

Prime Brokerage

Because hedge funds account for an increasingly large percentage of total trading volume on Wall Street, their relationships with the investment banks and brokerage houses have become increasingly important. It is estimated that last year hedge funds were responsible for one quarter of all commissions at Wall Street investment banks.

Within an investment bank, prime brokerage is a department that provides tools, services, and systems to a hedge fund that are beneficial in helping the fund to successfully grow its business, attract capital and operate smoothly. The main components of prime brokerage are clearing trades, stock lending, cash management, reporting, trading technology and client service. Potential hedge fund investors also consider which prime broker a particular hedge fund is using important, as some have a better reputation than others.

Once a hedge fund signs on as a client with a prime broker, they get access to all other resources the bank might have to offer; these may include online research, contacts in investment banking, trading desks, office space, and so on. Because of all these value-added services, prime brokers have become an integral part of the hedge fund structure. Jobs in prime brokerage, especially relationship management positions, have direct contact with hedge fund clients on a daily basis. They are the contacts for the hedge funds that can help in resolving their operational, accounting, and other problems.

Typical prime broker services include:

• **Brokerage and trading services:** global trade execution, clearing, and settlement.

• **Custody services:** global custody, multi-currency management, and dividend payout.

• **Information services:** research, access to market information, and reporting.

• **Financing services:** margin financing, securities borrowing and lending facilities, access to repo trades, loans, collateral, equity swaps, etc.

• **Risk management services:** real-time trade and portfolio reporting, proprietary risk control and risk management systems.

- **Administrative services:** office space, computer systems and technology, lawyers, tax advisory, accountants, and secretaries. (Administrative services are used primarily by hedge fund start-ups.)

Relationship Manager

The relationship manager is a highly qualified specialist committed to understanding a hedge fund's operational issues and investment strategies. A relationship manager manages 10 to 15 hedge fund client relationships on average, ranging in size from $10 million to several billion dollars, each having their own unique strategy.

The relationship manager position requires a bachelor's degree and strong communication skills. In addition, relationship manager professionals must have a basic understanding of margin rules and requirements across complex products, trade settlement, corporate actions, deliveries and payments.

The primary goal of relationship managers is to gather information for their clients (the hedge funds). To do this, they work with specialized departments in the investment bank, such as a department that specializes in dividends or a department that specializes in margin. (These departments are found only in investment banks, not hedge funds. At hedge funds, the operations department obtains this information either through the reporting offered by prime brokers or by calling their relationship manager.)

This is a client service-oriented job with constant interaction with clients and internal departments. It is a great opportunity to network, build contacts and learn about different hedge funds and how they operate.

Relationship management positions at prime brokerages are generally found on job search boards. Also, knowing somebody in a hedge fund or a bank can lead you to this type of position. The starting salary can range from $50K to $80K. Compared to some other finance-related jobs which see rapid growth of salary and bonuses, however, this position sees much slower compensation growth.

Career path

The relationship management (RM) role is also sometimes referred to as client service representative. This is a great starting point for someone looking to get a foot in the door of the hedge fund industry. The position exposes you to hedge funds that are different sizes, have varying strategies and a variety of locations. The role involves daily interaction with different individuals at the hedge fund, primarily the operations and accounting staff, which allows the RM to understand the different dynamics of how hedge funds operate.

After a few years in this role, an RM can stay on the investment banking (sell-side) and be promoted to a supervisory promotion. The general structure at most investment banks is a standard ladder of promotions, starting out with vice president, then director and, finally, managing director. The pay ranges increase at every level, with the managing director making between $150K and $500K. The managing director in this role will have many years of experience and will handle the client relationship on a macro level, getting away from day-to-day interactions. The managing director manages several RMs or client service reps and gets involved when there are more complex or difficult inquiries made by hedge fund clients. It is also the responsibility of the managing director to build and maintain strong relationships with the clients.

RMs also frequently leave the job to work for one of their clients or another hedge fund in operational roles. Hedge funds find the prime brokerage experience very valuable because of the multi-faceted issues that a RM deals with. These salaries are comparable to the hedge fund operational jobs discussed earlier.

Our Survey Says: Prime Brokerage

To help you get a sense of life as a hedge fund professional, Vault brings you the inside scoop via insiders in the industry.

Communication skills are paramount

Hector, 30 – "I have been working in client service roles for several years and I have found the most important aspect of being successful at it is communication skills. I have to be clear, concise and professional every time I am speaking with clients. Any conversation can be misconstrued and cause big problems. Just the other day, a client called about a notice we sent out about an upcoming voluntary issue where the shareholder of the particular security had the option of selling their shares at a certain price. After the client received this notice, I asked him if he was going to take action on it. He thought that I was asking him to participate in the issue. We have to be very careful what we say and how we say it. We can never say anything that can be interpreted as our giving advice to the client."

Great internship

Priya, 22 – "My senior year of college I interned in the prime brokerage department, and I have found the experience to be invaluable. I never really got around to talking to clients directly but I sat next to some RMs and learned many things, such as different security products, how the settlement process happens and what hedge funds are. After graduation I applied for a full-time position and got it. Now I've been here six months and I really enjoy what I am doing. I still have a huge learning curve ahead of me, but I always find myself using the things I learned during my internship. My manager told me that they generally do not hire right out of college, although my case was different because of the impression I made on them during my internship. To anyone trying to get into this industry, I recommend starting early and looking for internships your junior and senior year of college."

A Day in the Life: Prime Brokerage Relationship Manager

8:00 a.m.: Get into work. Check e-mail and daily trade breaks (client has a discrepancy in a trade vs. the executing broker). Immediately start reconciling trade breaks with each individual client (hedge funds).

9:00 a.m.: Work on making sure each client's portfolio looks accurate and see if there are any regulatory margin calls for the client. Examples include: shorts/longs in correct place, proper allocation of shares between various funds, Reg T, fed margin calls. Make sure all trade breaks and other position questions are communicated to the client (especially the trader/portfolio manager) prior to market open.

9:30 a.m.: Markets open. Field a variety of calls from clients with various strategies and proactively assess each client's technology and reporting needs.

10:00 a.m.: More calls. Each RM can typically have anywhere between five to 15 clients with a broad range in size (from a start-up hedge fund with $1 million to $1 billion assets under management). Clients keep steadily sending a stream of inquiries via phone and e-mail.

11:00 a.m.: On a call with a client inquiring regarding a good contact to trade short term Treasuries, while sending an e-mail to a client asking their liability for a right offering (type of re-org) for shares that they are short in their portfolio.

12:00 p.m.: An existing client calls and indicates he is interested in opening a new account with a risk arb strategy. He is requesting enhanced leverage vs. the standard 2:1.

12:30 p.m.: Work as liaison between margin, risk, and the new accounts department to provide the client with the accurate answers. After reporting the answers, you open a new account for him.

1:00 p.m.: Go get food and eat at desk while reading up on latest industry news announcements, particularly pertaining to hedge funds. Be able to multi-task and field client's calls as well.

3:00 p.m.: Work with all internal departments to ensure client satisfaction.

4:30 p.m.: Make sure all client trades get processed accurately and conduct several conference calls since client is done trading his portfolio.

5:30 p.m.: Meet client (hedge fund). Take the director of operations, CFO, COO and/or CEO out to a dinner, drinks and /or sports events. RMs typically entertain their clients several times a month.

9:30 p.m.: Head home to rest for the night.

FINAL ANALYSIS

Final Analysis

Hedge funds are unique and rapidly growing alternative investment vehicles. Back in 2003, the chairman of the SEC estimated that hedge funds would be a trillion-dollar industry by 2010. They reached that level some time in 2005.

This guide just scratches the surface of this complex industry. Many advanced books go in depth into the finance behind the strategies and many trading books speak to the experience that is necessary to become a hedge fund manager. As a guide for the novice, this book serves to assist you in determining whether this is the career for you and to help you with the interview process.

You should now be able to answer:

1. What are hedge funds?

2. How do hedge funds work and operate?

3. How do hedge funds make money?

4. Who are the key players at hedge funds?

5. How are hedge funds organized?

6. What are the different types of jobs available at hedge funds?

7. How do I research jobs?

8. What will the interview process be like? and much more. ...

Once you have decided what role interests you, you need to research the companies and potential job opportunities available. As discussed, there are many ways that you can learn about the industry and opportunities, including professional organizations, student organizations, networking, databases and the industry web sites.

You may be wondering, what are the future trends of hedge funds? Will this be a long-term industry that I can have a great career in? When the first edition of this book came out, that future was clouded by the potential of heavy regulation from the U.S. Securities and Exchange Commission, which grew wary of the massive amounts of capital controlled by hedge funds—which had very little regulatory oversight. In 2003, under SEC Chairman William Donaldson, the SEC issued an extensive report on the industry, with SEC staff recommending a number of measures to increase oversight of the relatively unregulated—some would say underregulated—industry.

Visit the Vault Finance Career Channel at **www.vault.com/finance** — with insider firm profiles, message boards, the Vault Finance Job Board and more.

VAULT CAREER LIBRARY   143

In 2006, the SEC finally took action, requiring all hedge funds to register as investment advisors under the Securities Act of 1993. Many hedge fund companies had already registered as such, voluntarily welcoming regulatory scrutiny, in part to assure would-be investors that their operations were above board. Now, however, nearly every hedge fund must register as advisors. That means funds have to open their books to the SEC—sometimes in random inspections—and also must have a chief compliance officer.

This doesn't mean, however, that the funds themselves are open to scrutiny. That point was very important to hedge funds, whose holdings and trading strategies were the core differential between funds. Exposing the "secret sauce" of fund operations would limit the impact these trading strategies could have. "Hedge funds take advantage of inconsistencies and minute opportunities throughout the broader markets," says one chief investment officer of a large fund. "If we had to detail how we were doing that, then everyone would try to exploit those little quirks in the market, and there wouldn't be as much money to be made."

The new SEC regulations do have a few loopholes. Funds with less than $30 million under management aren't required to register. Funds that lock up investors' money for two years or more are also immune from registration, as are funds that refuse to take on new investors. Given the growth of the industry and the increasing desire on investors' part to see their money freed up more often, a few funds have taken advantage of these loopholes.

The SEC still plans to keep a close eye on the industry, especially with notable problems of funds like Amaranth and Pirate periodically fueling calls for even more regulation. Hedge funds are constantly lobbying government to ensure their relative regulatory freedom. The current SEC, under Chairman Christopher Cox, is considered unlikely to make any wholesale changes in hedge fund oversight. The result of the 2008 elections may change that policy, but only somewhat. Hedge fund founders and even run-of-the-mill hedge fund employees (if there are such a thing) have become increasingly active in the political sphere, backing candidates on both sides of the aisle.

The regulatory battles will continue, certainly, but unlike a few years ago, hedge funds have garnered increasing acceptance. Pension funds, college endowments and other major private funds have invested in hedge funds, giving them a certain legitimacy in the marketplace. Even former Federal Reserve Chairman Alan Greenspan noted before his retirement that hedge funds often provide liquidity in otherwise illiquid markets, and had a positive role to play in tamping down volatility because of their hedging strategies.

Wall Street has also recognized hedge funds as an increasingly vital part of the marketplace. As we mentioned previously, nearly every major investment bank now has an internal hedge fund, and many have invested in private hedge fund companies as well. Hedge funds have also provided loans to major companies, both public and private, and have participated in leveraged buyouts alongside traditional private equity firms. Indeed, if hedge funds continue their growth and diversification, they may begin to look more and more like traditional Wall Street firms, and those traditional firms may start to look more like hedge funds as they expand their proprietary trading strategies and external investments.

Hedge fund careers are more dynamic than ever before, and the expertise required by individual funds is becoming more varied. These careers remain very fast-paced and continue to be at the very cutting edge of financial services. After reading this book and figuring out what appeals to you, the challenging high-paced world of hedge funds could be an exciting new career for you.

APPENDIX

Appendix

Recommended Reading

Books

You Can be a Stock Market Genius: Uncover the Secret Hiding Place of Stock Market Profits by Joel Greenblatt

Security Analysis, by Benjamin Graham and David Dodd

Value Investing: From Graham to Buffett and Beyond, by Bruce Greenwald

Hedge Funds: Investment and Portfolio Strategies for the Institutional Investor by Jess Lederman

When Genius Failed: The Rise and Fall of Long-Term Capital Management by Roger Lowenstein

Inventing Money: The Story of Long-Term Capital Management and the Legends Behind It by Nicholas Dunbar

Market Neutral Investing: Long/Short Hedge Fund Strategies by Joseph Nicholas

The Complete Arbitrage Deskbook by Steven Reverre

Risk Arbitrage by Keith Moore

Financial Shenanigans: How to Detect Accounting Gimmicks & Fraud in Financial Reports by Howard Schilit

Global Convertible Investing: The Gabelli Way

Creating Value Through Corporate Restructuring: Case Studies in Bankruptcies, Buyouts, and Breakups by Stuart Gilson

The Vulture Investors, Revised and Updated by Hilary Rosenberg

The Fundamentals of Hedge Fund Management: How to Successfully Launch and Operate a Hedge Fund, Daniel A. Strachman, Wiley Finance, 2007

The Hedge Fund Compliance and Risk Management Guide, Armelle Guizot, Wiley Finance, 2006

Hedge Fund Investment Management, Izzy Nelkin (Ed.), Elsevier Finance, 2005

How to Create and Manage a Hedge Fund, Stuart A. McCrary, Wiley Finance, 2002

Inside the House of Money: Top Hedge Fund Traders on Profiting in the Global Markets, Steven Drobny, Wiley, 2006

Investment Strategies of Hedge Funds, Filippo Stefanini, Wiley Finance, 2006

U.S. Regulations of Hedge Funds, Shartsis Friese, American Bar Association, 2006

Visit the Vault Finance Career Channel at **www.vault.com/finance** — with
insider firm profiles, message boards, the Vault Finance Job Board and more.

VAULT CAREER LIBRARY   **149**

News Articles

Anderson, Jenny and Julie Creswell, "Make Less Than $240 Million? You're Off Top Hedge Fund List," The New York Times, April 24, 2007, pg. A1

Crutsinger, Martin, "Bernanke says current system best for hedge fund regulations," The Associated Press, April 11, 2007

Fox, Justin, "Hedge Funds Head for Mediocrity," Time, Feb. 12, 2007, pg. 54

Goldstein, Matthew, "Hedge Funds Jump Into Private Equity," Business Week, Feb. 26, 2007, pg. 46

Goldstein, Matthew and Steve Rosenbush, "Hedge Fund Fees: The Pressure Builds," Business Week, May 14, 2007, pg. 40

Gordon, Marcy, "Wealthy hedge fund managers step up Washington activism as tax rumblings grow," The Associated Press, May 11, 2007

Kiviat, Barbara, "Hello, Hedge Funds," Time, Dec. 4, 2006, pg. 62

Lueck, Sarah, "Senate Aides Weight Hedge-Fund Tax Changes," The Wall Street Journal, March 15, 2007, pg. C3

Maxey, Daisy, "Wealthy Americans Cut Hedge Fund Risk," The Wall Street Journal, Jan. 25, 2007, pg. B1

Sender, Henny, "Hedge Funds' Risky Bets Come Home to Roost," The Wall Street Journal, March 8, 2007, pg. C1

Timmons, Heather, "Hedge Funds, the Usual Suspects, Blamed for Volatility in Asia," The New York Times, March 15, 2007, pg. C1

Vardi, Nathan, "Sewer Pipes," Forbes, Feb. 12, 2007, pg. 64

Werdigier, Julia, "It's Personal Up in the Stratosphere," The New York Times, May 1, 2007, pg. C10

Zuckerman, Gregory, "Big Hedge Funds Get Bigger, Leaving Less For Small Rivals," The Wall Street Journal, April 19, 2007, pg. C1

Zuckerman, Gregory, "Despite Bumps, Hedge Funds Push On," The Wall Street Journal, Jan. 2, 2007, pg. R15

Web Resources

Hedge Fund Center
http://www.hedgefundcenter.com

Hedgeworld
http://www.hedgeworld.com

Van Hedge Fund Advisors
www.vanhedge.com

The Wall Street Journal
www.wsj.com

Tremont Advisors
www.tassresearch.com

Visit the Vault Finance Career Channel at **www.vault.com/finance** — with
insider firm profiles, message boards, the Vault Finance Job Board and more.

VAULT CAREER LIBRARY   151

Investor Words
www.investorwords.com

Self-Reported Profiles of Top Hedge Funds

AIG Global Investment Group

70 Pine St.
New York, NY 10270
Phone: (800) 706-6661
Fax: (212) 770-9491
www.aiggig.com

Chairman & CEO: Win J. Neuger

CFO, Business Management: Brian P. McLoone

Senior Managing Director & Head of Business Development: Steven Guterman

Assets under Management: $8.1 billion in assets

Investment Strategy: The Hedge Fund Strategies Group seeks to identify and invest with the best managers in the hedge fund industry. We conduct an in-depth fundamental analysis of all managers, perform proactive quantitative and qualitative research and continuously monitor and adhere to a disciplined exit strategy. We believe in active management, data-driven research and thorough due-diligence through a top-down, bottom-up approach. The team adheres to an established and rigorous investment process to determine the suitability of new investments and to monitor existing ones.

No. of Office Locations (Worldwide): 45

No. of Employees (Hedge Fund division): 23 investment professionals. Over 100 Global

Employment Contact: hedgeinfo@aig.com

Investment Process

The teams' investment process consists of the following four major components:

• Manager Selection
• Asset and Strategy Allocation
• Portfolio Construction

• Risk Management

To be able to build a successful multi-manager program, AIGGIG strives to ensure access to the best managers on a global basis. Manager selection is one of the most important aspects of our process for driving alpha. AIGGIG views hedge funds as a "talent pool" of managers, not an asset class. We believe that talent drives performance. We seek talented individuals who trade on an information edge and capitalize on inefficiencies in the market. A single strategy often includes multiple asset classes, cross-market trades and various trading techniques. Therefore, we are constantly searching for "alpha hunters" that can attain strong performance.

Hiring Process:

The AIGGIG Hedge Fund Strategies Group screens approximately 500 fund managers on an annual basis. Typically, only 10% of the managers based on the below criteria make it to the due diligence phase.

For the approximate 10% of managers who pass the initial screening, we then conduct extensive quantitative and qualitative manager research, including onsite visits and analysis of performance and risk statistics. The few remaining managers are then visited by our "Manager Research Team" for evaluative meetings. Site visits involve extensive due diligence on the manager and his team, a thorough operational and risk management review and a performance analysis/quantitative review. Investment strategy, risk controls, track record, depth and quality of team and administration are evaluated. All "high priority managers," who pass must then also be approved by our Manager Selection Committee. Once selected, we continue to proactively monitor all managers.

Additional Information

Asset and Strategy Allocation

A properly structured multi-manager strategy may offer the potential for high absolute returns, while complementing traditional asset classes and improving portfolio risk/return optimization. The team combines a strategic "top-down" approach with a tactical "bottom-up" approach to analyse and determine optimal asset allocation. Additionally, the proposed allocations must then be approved by the nine senior-level members who comprise the Asset and Strategic Allocation Committee.

Portfolio Construction

Construction of a client's portfolio is determined by mixing the right amount of all the ingredients. Once the team has assessed the client's objectives, determined the expected return and risk of the strategy and selected the approved manager, the team applies a "best of breed" screening through qualitative and quantitative analysis and determines the optimal multi-manager portfolio to meet the client's needs.

Risk Management

As an integral part of the AIG culture, we strongly believe that risk must be managed proactively rather than reactively. Therefore, we carefully track various risk factors for each strategy and underlying fund. The hedge team constantly measures risk through ongoing risk management and monitoring procedures, both qualitative and quantitative. Through diligent, thorough and consistent analysis of data and statistics, the team ensures quality and relative safety.

Andor Capital Management

153 E. 53rd St., 58th Fl.
New York, NY 10022
Phone: (212) 224-5800
Fax: (212) 224-5800
www.andorcap.com

Firm Type: Private Company
Chairman and CEO: Daniel C. (Dan) Benton
Principal, Head of Marketing and Investor Relations: Julia B. Dailey
Managing Director and CFO: Peter G. Streinger
Assets under Management: $3 billion
No. of Office Locations (Worldwide): offices located in Greenwich, CT; San Mateo, CA and Taiwan
Employment Contact: humanresources@andorcap.com

Additional Information

Boolean Logic

Andor derives its name from Boolean Logic, an algebraic system developed by nineteenth century mathematician George Boole. In Boolean algebra variables must have one of two values: true or false; and relationships between variables are expressed with logical operators: AND, OR and NOT. Given these variables and the relationships they can have to one another, Boolean Logic is widely applied to process information and to solve problems. Readily applied to digital computing, Boolean operators are arranged, with the output from one providing input to another so that the final result is a reliable and meaningful conclusion.

As in Boolean algebra, our philosophy centers on established tenets that allow us to logically process information-determining fundamentals, eliminating sentiment, and arriving at a reliable and meaningful investment decision.

Angelo, Gordon & Co.

245 Park Ave.
New York, NY 10167
Phone: (212) 692-2000
Fax: (212) 867-9328
www.angelogordon.com

Firm Type: Private Company
CEO: John M. Angelo
COO and Chief Investment Officer: Michael L. Gordon
CFO: Joseph (Joe) Wekselblatt
Assets under Management: approximately $11 billion
No. of Employees (Hedge Fund division): 140 firmwide

Additional Information

Angelo, Gordon & Co. is a privately-held registered investment advisor dedicated to alternative investing. The firm was founded in 1988. We seek to generate absolute returns with low volatility by exploiting inefficiencies in selected markets and capitalizing on situations that are not in the mainstream of investment opportunities. We creatively seek out new opportunities that allow us to remain a leader in alternative investments.

We have expertise in a broad range of absolute return strategies for both institutional and high net worth investors. Our dedicated team of employees has enabled us to deliver consistent, positive returns over a long period in all market environments. We have built our name on our breadth of talent, intensive research and risk-averse approach to investing. Our long-term experience gives us the insight and patience to turn our vision into profitable, stable businesses.

Arden Asset Management

375 Park Avenue, 32nd Floor
New York, NY 10152
Phone: (212) 751-5252
Fax: 212-751-8546
www.ardenasset.com

CEO and President: Averell H. Mortimer
Managing Directors: Stephen C. Cordy and Ian McDonald
Assets under Management: Over $12 billion
Investment Objectives:
  • Consistent, high risk-adjusted returns
  • Low beta and overall correlation to traditional asset classes
  • Diversification across strategies and managers
  • Preservation of capital in adverse markets
  • Investments in controlled risk strategies, principally
  • Relative Value & Event-Driven
No. of Office Locations (Worldwide): principal offices in New York, London, and Singapore

Additional Information

Arden employs a disciplined and systematic four stage research-driven process that has been carefully refined over 10 years, in managing fund of hedge fund portfolios, which are designed with the intent of producing consistent performance results with low correlation to the global equity and fixed income markets.

MANAGER SOURCING
  • Proprietary sources, referrals, professional & personal relationships
  • Quantitative & qualitative screen of 7,000 + funds
  • 1,000 funds graduate to proprietary database for further analysis

DUE DILIGENCE
- Over 1,000 on-site manager visits per year
- In-depth manager due diligence to identify top managers
- Extensive operational review and background checks
- Investment committee approval of managers before investment

Atticus Capital

152 W 57th St.
New York, NY 10019
Phone: (212) 373-0800

Chairman and CEO: Timothy Barakett
Senior Managing Director: David Slager
Vice Chairman: Nathaniel Rothschild
Assets under management: $13 billion
No. of office locations: headquartered in New York with an office in London

Avenue Capital

535 Madison Ave
New York, New York 10022
Phone: 212-878-3535
www.avenuecapital.com

Partners: Marc Lasry and Sonia E. Gardner
Assets under Management: approximately $13.3 billion as of February 28, 2007
Investment Strategy: Avenue's goal in each strategy is to maximize returns while limiting risk and volatility. This is accomplished through in-depth research, disciplined investment philosophies and a consistent investment approach employed by experienced investment professionals.
No. of Office Locations (Worldwide): Headquartered in New York, with offices in London, Luxembourg, and eight offices throughout Asia
No. of Employees (Hedge Fund division): more than 245 employees firmwide
Employment Contact Info: www.avenuecapital.com/careers.htm

Blackstone Alternative Asset Management

345 Park Ave Fl 30

New York, NY 10154

Phone: 212-583-5000

Firm Type: Private Company

Senior Chairman and Co-Founder: Peter G. Peterson

Chairman, CEO and Co-Founder: Stephen A. Schwarzman

President, COO and Director: Hamilton E. (Tony) James

Managing Director: Edwin Conway

Assets under Management: approximately $18.4 billion

No. of Employees (firmwide): 770

Employment Contact: www.blackstone.com/careers

Recruiting

Our primary goal is to recruit top-tier candidates, challenge their thinking, cultivate their talent, and ultimately help them succeed. The key to remaining relevant and dynamic in the market place is recruiting and retaining superior talent. This is the hallmark of our Analyst and Associate Full-Time and Summer Internship Programs.

Hiring Process

Blackstone is seeking energetic, self-motivated, team-oriented individuals with fresh ideas and innovative solutions who thrive on challenge in a fast-paced, dynamic environment. Candidates should have excellent interpersonal and communication skills and should be strong group facilitators as well as capable leaders and successful team players. These traits are vital to our maintaining an atmosphere of intellectual challenge, mutual respect, acceptance and support.

Blackstone visits leading universities around the world in search of superior talent. We recruit individuals from diverse cultures and backgrounds. While your academic record is important to us, it is only one piece of the puzzle. What you bring to the table as an individual is equally as important.

We hire undergraduate and MBA candidates into our Analyst and Associate programs, respectively. Candidates are selected based on superior academic record and class ranking, degree of interest, work experience and level of ambition. A strong work ethic, entrepreneurial spirit, the ability to work in a team environment and a desire to learn are also key. Prior experience in the financial services industry is preferred, but not required. The number of hires sought each year varies, depending on market performance and the firm's expected growth.

Summer internships

Our summer recruiting process begins in January at our target schools, including receptions and/or dinners with our recruiting team. Such events are followed by formal interviews, both on and off-campus. Please check with your Career Services office to determine if yours is one of our target schools and, if so, when we will be visiting your campus. Unfortunately, Blackstone representatives cannot visit every school. If we do not conduct on-campus interviews at your school, please submit your resume via the link below and someone will contact you directly if you have been selected for further discussions with one of our groups.

After first round interviews are concluded, selected students are invited to our New York office for a multi-round process during which you will meet one-on-one with various members of the group to which you are applying.

Candidates who receive an offer will begin their summer employment in early June. The Internship Program is approximately 10 weeks in length.

The recommended timing to apply for a summer position is early December of your junior year. Summer Analyst Internships are for rising seniors only.

Visit the Vault Finance Career Channel at **www.vault.com/finance** — with
insider firm profiles, message boards, the Vault Finance Job Board and more.

VAULT CAREER LIBRARY   **159**

Inside the firm: culture and training

We offer a challenging, fast-paced yet collegial environment developed through teamwork and close working relationships with Blackstone's Senior Managing Directors. You will be given extensive responsibilities and will be stretched intellectually. We empower our people to exceed their own expectations.

Brevan Howard Asset Management

2nd Floor Almack House
London, England
Phone: +44-2078886429
www.brevanhoward.com

Bridgewater Associates

One Glendinning Place
Westport, CT 06880
Phone: 203.226.3030
Fax: 203.291.7300
www.bwater.com

Founder, President & Chief Investment Officer: Ray Dalio
CEO: Britt Harris
Assets under Management: $165 billion
Number of office locations: based in Westport, Connecticut
Number of Employees (firmwide): 350
Employment Contact: www.bwater.com/careers

Hiring Process

The key to our success is finding those rare, revolutionary thinkers - regardless of professional experience - who consistently challenge how things are done while inventing better ways to do them. People who work at Bridgewater have been selected because they have been high achievers (i.e. exceeded the standards of the general population).

Corporate Culture

Our culture requires: great people, shared mission to pursue, excellence at all costs, extreme openness to get at the truth and community.

"Another ingredient for success is team spirit. By team spirit, I am referring to 1) one's recognition of the responsibilities one has to help the team achieve its common goals and 2) the willingness to help others (i.e. work within a group) toward these common goals. This involves the realization that Bridgewater is a community in which our fates are intertwined. For the company to be successful every area of the company must work very well; if one area fails, the system breaks down. As the saying goes, we are as strong as our weakest link, and this is why the individual must recognize his or her importance and obligations to the whole organization. When this behavior exists, people also know that others can be relied on to go to extraordinary lengths to help. As a corollary, substandard performance cannot be tolerated anywhere in the company because it would hurt everyone. Poor performance and/or uncooperative attitudes undermine the team. One of the most difficult responsibilities a team leader has is to cut poor performers, particularly those who are trying but don't have the ability. This is often perceived harsh or unkind, but it is ultimately best for everyone, including the person who is being cut. Think of Bridgewater as being a team like the Green Bay Packers under Vince Lombardi - if you like being challenged and performing up to your potential, Bridgewater is the right place for you. If you are thin-skinned and don't like conflict or criticism, you should be somewhere else."

— Ray Dalio

Addtional information

We believe the best way to manage money is to separate investment alpha (value-added return from active management) from beta (return from passively holding a portfolio) and then create optimal portfolios of each. At Bridgewater, we manage money for clients across most major asset classes by replicating a client benchmark and overlaying the benchmark with our optimal alpha strategy, Pure Alpha®. Clients specify their desired targeted level of risk.

To generate alpha, we follow a fundamental and systematic investment process. By fundamental, we seek to understand the timeless and universal influences on global markets. By systematic, we pre-specify all of our investment criteria, allowing us to debate and test their merits and implement decisions with objectivity and thoroughness. This process gives us the ability to make better decisions and create more diversified portfolios, producing more consistent performance.

Campbell & Co.

210 West Pennsylvania Avenue Suite 770
Towson, MD 21204
Phone: (800) 698.7235
Fax: 410.296.3311
www.campbell.com

Founder: Keith Campbell

CEO: Edith H. Falk

Investment Strategy: For more than three decades, Campbell & Company has built and sustained a competent business through the successful provision of absolute return strategies for sophisticated investors. While it is essential to recognize that past results are not indicative of future performance, we are determined to improve upon our abilities, and we work tirelessly in an attempt to provide consistent, attractive risk-adjusted returns.

Our trading decisions are based upon proprietary trading models designed to detect and exploit medium- to long-term price changes. We invest in a multitude of markets and instruments including global interest rates, equities, stock indices, currencies, energy and assorted commodities. We use futures, forward and option contracts as well as long and short positions to capture trends or exploit inefficiencies in the markets. All of the markets in which we trade have a high degree of liquidity and transparency.

Our portfolios incorporate multiple strategies. When combined, these strategies deliver broad diversification designed to help mitigate risk.

Risk management tools are integral to our models, providing our first defense against losses. Additional risk monitoring, measurement and management tools are employed regularly to reduce risk and attempt to preserve capital in each portfolio. While there have been periods during which our clients have incurred losses, this disciplined approach has generally provided our clients with consistent returns during the last thirty-four years

Corporate Culture

At Campbell & Company people are our priority. Since inception, we have been distinguished by our ability to attract exceptional talent in every aspect of our business.

Our culture encourages creativity, productivity and loyalty - key qualities that we seek in our business partners, and that we credit to our success

No. of Office Locations (Worldwide): principal offices in New York, London, and Singapore

Caxton Associates

731 Alexander Rd
Princeton, NJ 08540
Phone: 609-419-1800
www.caxton.com

Founder: Bruce Kovner
Assets under management: $14 billion
No. of Employees (Hedge Fund division): 350 people, including traders, research analysts and administrative personnel in its offices in New York, Princeton, NJ and London
Employment Contact Info: E-mail: employment@caxton.com

Cerberus Capital Management

299 Park Ave.
New York, NY 10171
Phone: (212) 891-2100
Fax: (212) 891-1540
www.cerberuscapital.com

Firm Type: Private Company
Chairman: John W. Snow
CEO & Senior Managing Director: Steven A. Feinberg
Senior Managing Director: William L. Richter
Senior Managing Director and COO: Mark A. Neporent

Investment Strategy: At Cerberus, we have a long-term investment horizon and focus on value creation. We invest in undervalued companies and their people, and help them to realize their potential.

We partner with our portfolio companies to help them become industry leaders. We believe competition makes the global economy more productive and more efficient, which enables companies to succeed long-term in the globally competitive marketplace.

We encourage our companies to focus on the future through prudent capital investment, R&D, new product marketing, talent development, improved operations and appropriate strategic acquisitions.

No. of Office Locations (Worldwide): advisory offices in Atlanta, Chicago, Los Angeles, London, Baarn, Frankfurt, Tokyo, Osaka and Taipei

No. of employees (firmwide): about 275 investment and operations professionals

Citadel Investment Group

131 S. Dearborn St.
Chicago, IL 60603
Phone: (312) 395-2100
Fax: (312) 977-0270
www.citadelgroup.com

Firm Type (Private, Public, etc.): Private Company
Managing Director and CEO: Kenneth C. (Ken) Griffin
CFO: Gerald Beeson
CIO: Thomas G. (Tom) Miglis
No. of Office Locations (Worldwide): Chicago (HQ), Hong Kong, London, New York, San Francisco and Tokyo
Employment Contact:
Please address your correspondence to:

College Recruiting
Citadel Investment Group, L.L.C.
131 South Dearborn Street
Chicago, IL 60603
USA

Undergraduate, Masters and Ph.D. Candidates:
collegerecruiting@citadelgroup.com

MBA Candidates:
mbarecruiting@citadelgroup.com

Experienced Hire Candidates:
exprecruiting@citadelgroup.com

Career web site address:
www.citadelgroup.com/careers

Recruiting

Opportunities for College Graduates
Citadel offers an exciting and challenging environment. If you share our drive and passion, there is no better place to build your career.

Citadel is a highly integrated organization, and each part of the business plays a critical role in contributing to our outstanding record. We offer challenging opportunities for undergraduate, masters, MBA and Ph.D. candidates in the following areas:

- Investments and Trading
- Quantitative Research
- Information Technology
- Financial Accounting and Operations
- Entry-level positions are available in Chicago, our worldwide headquarters.

Hiring Process

Undergraduate/Masters Candidates

Each candidate interviewed on campus will have two consecutive 30-minute interviews. This one-hour format will allow Citadel to assess both qualitative and technical skills and acumen. A member of the college recruiting team will contact each candidate via email within seven days regarding the status of his/her candidacy. Should a candidate be invited to continue the interview process with Citadel, all subsequent interviews will take place at Citadel's worldwide headquarters in Chicago.

MBA Candidates

Each candidate interviewed on campus will have one 45-minute interview conducted by two Citadel professionals. A member of the college recruiting team will contact each candidate via email within seven days regarding the status of his/her candidacy. Should a candidate be invited to continue the interview process with Citadel, all subsequent interviews will take place at Citadel's worldwide headquarters in Chicago.

Upon extending your offer, we are confident that we have invited one of the best and brightest graduates to join the Citadel team. You represent our future - congratulations! At Citadel, you will work alongside some of the most brilliant minds in the industry. Our goal is to provide the most rewarding career opportunity available in the world of financial services and investment management.

It is important to make the decision that is best for you when considering the job offer. Bear in mind the following factors when evaluating the offers you receive from prospective employers:

Visit the Vault Finance Career Channel at **www.vault.com/finance** — with insider firm profiles, message boards, the Vault Finance Job Board and more.

VAULT CAREER LIBRARY   **165**

Role

• Growth Potential
• Technology
• Infrastructure

We believe that when you consider these factors you will determine that Citadel is the best choice for you and your career. Please remember that your recruiter and future colleagues are available to assist you with any questions.

Role:
• Do you have a full understanding of how you will be integrated into the business?
• Can you picture yourself collaborating with the team members?
• Do you feel intellectually stimulated when considering the components of the role?
• Do you see yourself being successful in a fast-paced, dynamic environment?

Growth Potential:
• Does the firm provide growth opportunities for the future?
• Do you see the potential to grow your own career?
• Are you aware of employees with similar backgrounds growing into leadership roles?
• Does the firm provide opportunities for professional development and continuing education?

Technology:
• Will you be sitting alongside business leaders to develop technology that is readily implemented?
• Will you work with the most state-of-the art technology available to meet business needs?

Infrastructure
• Does the firm have the infrastructure necessary to compete with the best financial services firms in the world?
• Does it have the quantitative research team to create models, a technology team to design proprietary trading systems, and an operations team to settle all trades, collaborating together on a daily basis?
• Is the firm diversified such that it has the ability to be successful in any market condition?

• What are some of the requirements for jobs (GPA, degree, personality, skills, etc.)?

Investments and Trading: Successful candidates will demonstrate both an intense desire and a clear ability to use intellect to gain an edge over other participants in the financial markets. Knowledge of investments and financial markets is required. Previous work experience at a financial services institution is strongly desired. Qualified candidates come from a wide range of academic backgrounds including economics, finance, accounting, mathematics, physics, engineering and computer science.

Quantitative Research: Successful candidates will need strong software development skills, a thorough understanding of theoretical and empirical modeling, effective communication skills, and an ability to work effectively as part of an integrated team. Qualified candidates typically have or are in the pursuit of a Ph.D. in a quantitative discipline.

Information Technology: Successful candidates must have a thorough understanding of, and experience in, software development, with a degree in either engineering or computer science. Candidates must also demonstrate a strong interest in finance.

Financial Accounting and Operations: Successful candidates will have exceptional communication skills, an aptitude for solving problems, be detail- and process-oriented and have the ability to work effectively as part of an integrated team. Qualified candidates usually possess a degree in either accounting, finance or economics.

Summer internships

Citadel offers a 10-week summer internship program for exceptional students interested in a career in alternative investments. This comprehensive program provides students with the necessary foundation to apply classroom training to practice in the workplace.

The goal of Citadel's Summer Internship Program is to provide a realistic preview of the full-time opportunities available at Citadel. We are committed to developing you early in your career through project-based assignments designed to aide in your understanding of the industry while having an impact on the firm. The College Recruiting Team will partner with your assigned manager to outline the goals and expectations for a successful summer. The designated manager will review your progress throughout the duration of the summer program and provide continuous feedback via a formal review process.

To further support your development throughout the summer, an additional Citadel colleague will be provided as a resource to assist you in becoming acclimated to the environment, your co-workers, and our industry.

The internship program has three components: Summer Projects; Education Series; Team Building/Networking Events

The intern projects are specific to each individual and are driven by the current needs of the business. Citadel hosts an education series that highlights the different teams to provide you with a high-level understanding of the firm's investment strategies, infrastructure, and culture. You will also engage in team building activities that provide the opportunity to further develop your communication, leadership, and presentation skills. In addition, you will have multiple opportunities to network with colleagues in both formal and informal settings.

Internship opportunities are available in Chicago, our worldwide headquarters, to exceptional students within one year of graduation. If you are studying Computer Science, Computer Engineering, Electrical Engineering, Financial Engineering, Finance, Economics, Accounting, Mathematics or Physics at the undergraduate or graduate level, we encourage you to apply.

Compensation

Citadel places a strong emphasis on retaining its employees. Our world-class benefits package is just one aspect of Citadel's comprehensive compensation and benefits program.

Our outstanding benefits package has many components including but not limited to:
• Medical Plan
• Prescription Drug Plan
• Vision Plan
• Hearing Plan
• Dental Plan
• Retirement Savings Plan (401(k) with company match)
• Basic Life and Accidental Death & Dismemberment Insurance
• Short-Term Disability
• Long-Term Disability

• Travel Insurance
• Paid Time Off
• Education and Training Reimbursement
• Transit Benefits
• Back-Up Child Care

Corporate culture

Citadel is a place where incredibly talented people teach and learn from each other every day. We are committed to ongoing education and development.

From day one, you will be working alongside and learning from some of the best and brightest individuals in the industry. You will have access to classroom-based learning opportunities, and a significant part of your training will be on the job where immediate application of new principles will enable you to quickly extend your skills and take on new responsibilities.

Regularly scheduled training is available to all employees and is a critical component of our culture of learning. The Business Overview Program is a series of presentations intended to acquaint new employees with all aspects of the business. Monthly Brown Bag Lunches are conducted to inform employees of current Citadel-related topics and general hedge fund industry issues.

In addition, our world-class benefits package includes a tuition reimbursement program that provides substantial financial support to further your education and development. We also collaborate with leading experts in academia and industry to design and implement customized learning programs for our employees.

D. E. Shaw & Co.

120 W. 45th St., 39th Fl., Tower 45
New York, NY 10036
Phone: (212) 478-0000
Fax: (212) 478-0100
www.deshaw.com

Firm Type: Private Company
Chairman and CEO: David E. Shaw
Managing Director: Eric Wepsic
SVP Sales and Marketing: Robert Bartkowiak
No. of Office Locations (Worldwide): offices in New York, London, Silicon Valley, Houston, Kansas City, San Francisco, Washington, D.C., Bermuda, and Hyderabad and Gurgaon, India.
No. of Employees: 260
Employment Contact Info:
For recruiting-related inquiries:
recruiting-inquiries@world.deshaw.com

Career web site address:
www.deshaw.com/Recruiting.html

Recruiting

The D. E. Shaw group offers opportunities for individuals of all backgrounds and levels of experience who display evidence of outstanding ability and have a track record of exceptional accomplishment. We hire gifted mathematicians and computer scientists as well as extraordinary generalists with liberal arts or other non-technical backgrounds. (Some of the firm's managing directors hold degrees in fields as disparate as English, Psychology, and Russian Studies.) Many of our employees have little knowledge of finance when they join the firm, but all share uncommon intelligence, analytical ability, and drive.

Corporate culture

At the D. E. Shaw group you'll be working with people trained in a variety of disciplines in a collegial, casual environment in which corporate hierarchies are kept to a minimum. There is no dress code (you won't see many suits and ties), our vacation policy is flexible, and many positions don't have fixed hours. New hires often enjoy surprising amounts of responsibility, and we encourage collaboration, personal mentorships with senior team members, and the open exploration of ideas. As a result, many employees feel that the firm combines some of the most attractive features of academia with considerably greater rewards.

There are also abundant opportunities for rapid professional growth. One of our managing directors literally started in the mailroom, and it's not uncommon for people to move between departments if there's a fit for both the firm and the individual. Career paths are governed primarily by the evolution of an employee's interests and abilities.

DB Absolute Return Strategies

Phone: (212) 454 2118

https://ars.db.com/arsportal/index.jsp

Assets under Management: approximately $7.9 billion in hedge fund assets (as of 31 March 2007)
No. of Office Locations (Worldwide): offices in New York, London, Zurich, Bahrain, Tokyo and Singapore
No. of Employees (Hedge Fund division): 140
Employment Contact
Career website: www.db.com/careers

Hiring Process

Our prime objective is to hire the most intelligent, talented, highly qualified and motivated people from around the globe

Corporate culture

Our initiatives concentrate on:

- Enabling people to reconcile family and profession
- Boosting and maintaining health and capacity to work of all employees
- Being able to influence corporate culture positively

Summer internships

We recruit students from leading universities across the globe into our graduate and summer internship analyst programs

Compensation

Other monetary benefits (401(k), investment opportunities, stock options or purchase, etc.) include:

- Flexible Work arrangements
- Health check for executives
- Company doctor service
- Company sports clubs
- Preventative medical options from the company health insurance fund

Diversity

What is diversity at DB?
By diversity, we refer to the business attitude that encompasses respect, open-mindedness and a commitment to individual professional and personal growth. DB expects every employee to share this attitude. Encouraging our employees to celebrate their own diversity and that of their colleagues is fundamental to our corporate values and critical to our business success

Why is diversity important for DB?
Diversity manages differences in a respectful and valuing way and turns difference into competitive advantage for the business. This could mean to tap successfully into new markets and client groups because the organization understands how to deal with cultural, societal and historical differences through an empathetic, open-minded and understanding behaviour.

What evidence is there to demonstrate that the organization values diversity?
DB has an extensive range of initiatives that demonstrates the value placed upon diversity within the Bank. Initiatives are focused upon achieving our strategic goals outlined above, for which a diverse working environment is essential. These are supported by diversity training, a code of conduct and commitment from the Board to the 'One Bank' culture.

What are the goals of DB diversity strategy?
Diverse Workforce To have diverse representation of employees at all levels of the organization Inclusive Work Environment To have an inclusive work environment where individual and team effectiveness is maximized Diversity Leader To be seen as a Diversity leader in the financial industry and beyond by all Deutsche Bank stakeholders Leadership To have all managers lead and become accountable for driving Diversity as an integrated part of the business performance.

<u>What programs are in place to support minority groups?</u>

DB has a range of policies to support minority groups. These polices are embedded within DB's business practices. They range from searching out top talent, to providing supporting structures (e.g. employee networks), to networking opportunities (e.g. networking breakfasts), to events (e.g. WEB conference) and promoting diversity within DB'sore values.

<u>What diversity awards have Deutsche Bank won?</u>

In 2005 Deutsche won the Total E-Quality award for the 3rd time in succession. In 2003 DB on the Race for Opportunity Award as one of the 10 Most Improved Companies within the Private Sector and was listed in the 100 Best Companies for Working Mothers in the Working Mother Magazine. DB has also won awards in the US for its diversity programs e.g. listed in the top 10 Gay Friendly US Companies in The Advocate.

<u>Are the Bank's diversity policies only for internal employees?</u>

No, our diversity policies are intended to have a far reaching effect. They should impact upon our employees, clients, suppliers, shareholders, stakeholders and on the communities in which DB operates.

EIM

750 Lexington Avenue
New York, 10022
Phone: (212) 371-9000
Fax: (212) 371-9111
www.eimgroup.com

Firm Type: Private Company
No. of Office Locations (Worldwide): "Worldwide Presence" offices in Nyon, Germany; Zurich; London; New York; Paris; Gibraltar; Singapore and Monaco
No. of Employees (Hedge Fund division): More than 170 Employees

Fortress Investment Group

345 Avenue of the Americas
New York, NY 10105
Phone: (212) 798-6100
www.fortressinv.com

Firm Type (Private, Public, etc.): Public Company
Chairman and CEO: Wesley R. (Wes) Edens
Co-President and Director: Peter L. Briger Jr.
COO and Director: Randal A. Nardone
Assets under Management: $35.1 billion as of December 31, 2006
No. of Office Locations (Worldwide): affiliates with offices in Dallas, Frankfurt, Geneva, Hong Kong, London, Los Angeles, Rome, San Diego, Sydney and Toronto
No. of Employees: 400
Employment Contact:

Michele I. Cohen
Managing Director, Human Resources
Fortress Investment Group LLC
1345 York, NY 10105
E-mail: jobs@fortrssinv.com

ESL Investments

CEO: Edward S. "Eddie" Lampert

Grosvenor Capital Management
900 North Michigan Avenue
Suite 1100
Chicago, IL 60611
www.grosvenorcapitalmanagement.com
Phone: (312) 263-7777

Employment Contact Info: hr@gcmlp.com

Ivy Asset Management
1 Jericho Plz Ste 304
Jericho, NY 11753
Phone: (516) 545-8430
www.ivyasset.com

Co-Presidents: Michael E. Stinger and Sean G. Simon
Vice Chairmen: Larry Simon and Howard Wohl,
No. of Office Locations (Worldwide): Headquartered in New York, operations in Europe and Japan

Assets under management: $15.1 billion

Employment Contact

Liz Brunner

Director of Human Resources

E-mail: careers@ivyasset.com

Career web site address:

www.ivyasset.com/career_opportunities.aspx

Corporate culture

At Ivy Asset Management, a collegial culture is the foundation of our organization and the guiding principle for how we have conducted business since our inception. We believe there are no excuses for inappropriate behavior.

To establish such an environment, we are diligent in our hiring practices. We carefully identify talent not only with superior credentials but with the professional attitude necessary to maintain a culture of courtesy and respect. Each and every one of our employees - from executive to support staff - must treat one another with high esteem.

Since the earliest days of our company, Ivy Asset Management has always been committed to the highest principles of ethical and social behavior. This is reflected in the way we treat our employees, clients and partners in the workplace, the marketplace and the community.

Our commitment to corporate citizenship spans the business spectrum. This includes a host of activities, from human resource efforts that reflect work/life balance needs and promote diversity, to corporate governance practices that ensure a financial and management process of the utmost integrity.

We are also deeply committed to corporate philanthropy, viewing charitable giving as both an imperative and a privilege. To this end, we have established a formal charitable giving committee, comprised of representatives from across the firm to review proposals and determine contributions. Contributions are geared to charities that focus on humanitarian concerns, social welfare, and the issues of children, their health, and their families. In addition, we fund a host of non-profit institutions that play an active and important role in the local communities in which we operate.

We also encourage our employees to volunteer their time and services in their respective home communities. Since volunteerism is an important component of corporate citizenship, we are committed to supporting our professionals in their personal endeavors.

One of the key strengths of Ivy Asset Management is the leadership and experience of our management team. Combining the energies of a new generation of leadership with the wisdom of our founders, we ensure both a consistency of investment approach and firm culture with ongoing investments in new strategies and systems.

Diversity

The Bank of New York Company, Inc. and its subsidiaries provide equal employment opportunity to all qualified employees and applicants for employment regardless of race, color, creed, religion, sex, national origin, ancestry, citizenship status, age, marital status, sexual orientation, physical or mental disability, veteran status, liability for service in the Armed Forces of the United States, or any other classification prohibited by applicable law.

Additional information

Through its funds and advisory relationships, Ivy manages assets for a host of investors ranging from high-net-worth individuals to blue-chip institutional players. Our clientele includes:

- Fortune 500 companies
- Global and Money Center Banks
- Multi-National Insurance corporations
- Global Investment Banking firms
- Municipality Pension Plans
- Taft-Hartley Plans
- Offshore Entities
- Registered Investment Companies
- Foundations
- Endowments
- Non-profits
- Professional Money Managers
- High-Net-Worth Individuals
- Private Family Offices

Mesirow Advanced Strategies

350 N. Clark St.

Chicago, IL 60610

Phone: (312) 595-6000; (800) 453-0600

Fax: (312) 595-4246

www.mesirowfinancial.com

Chairman: Howard M. Rossman

CEO: Martin B. Kaplan

Assets under management: $22.2 billion

No. of Employees: 1,200 employees firmwide

Hiring Process

Our investment professionals possess excellent credentials including advanced academic, accounting and financial degrees.

Oaktree Capital Management, LLC

333 S. Grand Ave., 28th Fl.

Los Angeles, CA 90071

Phone: (213) 830-6300

Fax: (213) 830-6393

www.oaktreecapital.com

Firm Type: Private Company

Chairman: Howard S. Marks

President: Bruce A. Karsh

Principal, CFO, and Chief Administrative Officer: David M. Kirchheimer

Assets under management: approximately $35 million

Investment strategy: Excellence in investing, proprietary, in-depth research, commonality of interests, personnel practices, communication with clients, management fee arrangements, new products and profitability

No. of Offices: offices located in Los Angeles; Luxembourg; New York; Singapore; Stamford, CT; Tokyo; Frankfurt, Hong Kong and Beijing

No. of Employees (firmwide): 345

Corporate culture

Our personnel practices must contribute to the achievement of our clients' objectives. A harmonious workplace and a spirit of cooperation are indispensable; personnel turnover, office politics and unhealthy competition are to be guarded against. The fruits of our labor will always be shared broadly and equitably with our staff. Employee stock ownership and firm-wide profit participation are key in this.

Och-Ziff Capital Management

9 W 57th St Fl 39
New York, NY 10019
Phone: (212) 790-0120

Pacific Alternative Asset Management Co.

19540 Jamboree Road, Suite 400
Irvine, CA 92612
Phone: (949) 261 4900
Fax: (949) 261 4901
www.paamco.com

CEO: Jane Buchan
No. of Office Locations: offices in Irvine, CA and London

Pequot Capital Management

500 Nyala Farm Rd.
Westport, CT 06880
Phone: (203) 429-2200
Fax: (203) 429-2400
www.pequotcap.com

Firm Type: Private Company
Chairman and CEO: Arthur J. Samberg
Assets under management: $7.5 billion
No. of Office Locations (Worldwide): offices in Connecticut, New York, Massachusetts, California and London
No. of Employees (Hedge Fund division): 280 employees

Permal Group

900 3rd Ave Fl 28
New York, NY 10022
Phone: (212) 418 6500

www.permal.com

CEO: Isaac R. Souede

Assets under management: $27 billion

Investment Strategy: The goal of the multi-manager portfolios is to create and maintain diversified portfolios of quality managers that provide safety of capital, excellent investor liquidity and above average returns with below average volatility when compared with traditional investments. Permal portfolios are designed to participate significantly in strong markets, preserve capital in down or volatile markets and outperform market indices over a full market cycle. A market cycle can be defined as a combination of bullish and bearish periods. By diversifying assets by manager, region, investment style, asset class, and/or sector, we seek to reduce overall portfolio risk.

No. of Office Locations (Worldwide): principal offices in New York, London, and Singapore

Hiring Process

Manager selection is a comprehensive process which may involve any of the following criteria:

- Demonstrated ability to perform in up and down markets
- Solid experience and a proven track record
- Risk control systems implemented
- An edge to outperform the market averages
- Investment of manager's own capital, aligning manager risks with those of the client
- A stable organizational structure

Perry Capital

767 5th Ave Fl 19

New York, NY 10153

Phone: (212) 583-4000

www.perrycap.com

Assets under management: $13 billion

No. of Office Locations: offices in New York, Hong Kong and London

No. of Employees: over 140

Employment Contact:

For employment consideration, please forward your resume to:
Perry Capital
767 Fifth Avenue, 19th Floor
New York, NY 10153
Attention: Human Resources
Email: recruiting@perrycap.com

Pirate Capital LLC

200 Connecticut Ave., 4th floor
Norwalk, CT 06854
Phone: (203) 854-1100
www.piratecapitalllc.com

CEO: Tom Hudson
No. of Office Locations (Worldwide): principal offices in New York, London, and Singapore

Quellos Capital Management

601 Union St Fl 56
Seattle, WA 98101-2341
Phone: (206) 613-6700; (866) 613-6700
www.quellos.com

CEO: Jeff Greenstein
No. of Office Locations (Worldwide): principal offices in New York, London, and Singapore
Assets under Management: $15.6 billion
Investment Strategy: Quellos's approach to active investment management is predicated on the belief that portfolio managers can add value by selecting securities that will outperform a broadly diversified passive portfolio. Their absolute return strategies employ this 'value added' approach by specifically targeting market inefficiencies.

Employment Contact

Career web site address:
www.quellos.com/Careers.aspx

Hiring Process

Quellos is an employer of choice for dynamic, confident, bright, accomplished individuals who share common values of integrity, teamwork, innovation and a passion for continual improvement in the delivery of value-added financial solutions for our clients. Our diverse workforce is focused on client service and operational excellence.

Summer internships

In addition to regular employment opportunities, we offer selective Work Study and Summer Internship programs. Top university students will have a valuable learning experience with significant work assignments, project responsibilities and exposure to Quellos' core business. While Work Study opportunities are available throughout the year, Summer Intern selections normally occur in the January through March timeframe.

Soros Fund Management

888 7th Ave., 33rd Fl.
New York, NY 10106
Phone: 212-262-6300
Fax: 212-245-5154

Firm Type: Private Company
Chairman and President: George Soros
CFO and COO: Abbas F. (Eddy) Zuaiter
Assets under Management: $13 billion
Investment Strategy: The company's investment strategies have been based on analysis of real or perceived macroeconomic trends in various countries.

Tremont Capital Management

555 Theodore Fremd Avenue
Rye, NY 10580
Phone: (914) 925-1140
Fax: (914) 921-3499
www.tremont.com

CEO: Robert I. Schulman
President: Rupert Allan
Chief Investment Officer: Cynthia J. Nicoll

No. of Office Locations (Worldwide): offices in Rye, NY; London; Toronto and Hong Kong

No. of Employees: over 120 people in the United States, Canada, the United Kingdom, and Hong Kong

Investment strategy: The most important components of Tremont's investment process are:

- An emphasis on quantifying forward-looking views on manager and strategy returns and downside risks.
- A risk-focused framework for evaluating portfolios that gives us higher confidence in the returns we generate for a given level of downside risk.
- An understanding of risk as downside risk and not volatility, assessing both from investment and operational risk sources.
- The creation of optimal portfolios based on forward-looking views on returns and downside risks.
- The proper alignment of interests of all Investment Management professionals with the goal of generating the best set of future returns for a given level of downside risk.

Employment Contact

Tremont Group Holdings, Inc.
555 Theodore Fremd Avenue
Rye, New York 10580
Attention: Human Resources
Career website:
www.tremont.com/careers.aspx

Hiring Process

We seek experienced individuals capable of delivering a wide range of value-added services to our clients around the world, while helping them to confront today's critical issues head on.

Corporate culture

At Tremont, you can find challenging opportunities in an environment that recognizes and rewards exceptional performance.

Tudor Investment Corporation

1275 King St
Greenwich, Connecticut 06831
Phone: (203) 863-6700
Fax: (203) 863-8600
www.tudorfunds.com

Firm Type: Private Company
CEO: Paul T. Jones
Assets under Management: $16.8 billion
(as of March 1, 2007)
No. of Office Locations (Worldwide): Offices located in Boston, Massachusetts; Epsom, Surrey, United Kingdom; Greenwich, Connecticut (Corporate Headquarters and Administrative Office); London, United Kingdom; New York, New York; Singapore; Sydney, Australia and Washington D.C.
No. of Employees: 384 Employees
Employment Contact: E-mail: tradercareers@tudor.com

Recruiting

Tudor Investment Corporation actively seeks new investment managers to complement its existing team of over 50 portfolio managers operating in its offices in Greenwich, CT, Boston, New York, London, Surrey, Singapore and Sydney. With trading and investment capabilities in global commodity, currency, fixed income and equity markets, Tudor offers a platform which enables portfolio managers to focus exclusively on the development and implementation of trading and investment strategies.

Portfolio manager candidates applying for a position should have significant investment experience including a multi-year independent track record in their stated strategy.

Please forward all trading candidate position inquiries to tradercareers@tudor.com.

Tudor also recruits talented individuals to support our diversified trading business. For exceptional candidates with the right skill set, at any given time, we may have positions open in Operations, Middle Office, Technology, Risk Management, Financial Data, Corporate Financial Reporting, Tax, Legal, Compliance, Investor Relations, HR/Talent Management, Treasury and Facilities. Candidates with excellent qualifications can send resumes and cover letters to: careers@tudor.com.

Tudor offers a competitive benefits package and is an Equal Opportunity Employer.

Compensation

Compensation is formula-based.

Top Hedge Funds Organized by Specialty

The following hedge funds are categorized by their best-known strategies. Today, however, given the increasingly competitive industry, many fund companies offer investments in multiple strategies - and many fund managers are perfectly happy to grab opportunities as they see them, whether or not they technically fit in with the overall strategy.

Equities (Long/Short or Market-Neutral)

These funds invest in the stock market, but have the option of shorting stock as well as going long. Critics say there's little difference between these and traditional long/short mutual funds, but these funds can also engage in the equity options trade, and are generally far more nimble in their investments.

- Andor Capital Management
- Grosvenor Capital Management
- Superfund Group
- Tudor Investment Corp.

Arbitrage (Risk, Convertible or Multistrategy)

As explained earlier, arbitrageurs seek to take advantage of opposing moves in a variety of markets. Risk and merger arbitrage is common amongst stocks, but arbs also find opportunities in the movements between stocks and bonds, bonds and currencies - almost any number of asset classes.

- Citadel Investment Group
- Davidson Kempner Capital Management
- HBK Capital Management
- Och-Ziff Capital Management
- Renaissance Technologies Corp.

Macro

These hedge funds take advantage of shifts in global macroeconomics, particularly in a given nation's interest rate policy, which can affect bonds and currencies in particular.

- Caxton Associates
- D.E. Shaw & Co.
- Man Investments
- Fortress Investment Group
- Soros Fund Management

Distressed Companies and Debt

When companies are in trouble, these hedge funds attend the fire sale. Increasingly, these funds aren't just buying distressed debt or stocks on the cheap - they're buying whole companies and, in many ways, becoming de facto private equity firms. Cerberus' purchase of the Chrysler Group and ESL Investments buyout of Kmart are just two examples.

- Avenue Capital
- Cerberus Capital Management
- ESL Investments
- Oaktree Capital Management

Multistrategy

More and more, fund companies are simply classifying themselves as multistrategy; they'll do anything if there's money to be made. Some will create specific funds for each strategy they employ, while others will simply pool the money - merger arbitrage one day, a macro play on European currencies the next.

- Angelo, Gordon & Co.
- Ivy Asset Management
- Mesirow Advanced Strategies
- Pequot Capital Management
- Permal Group
- SAC Capital Advisors

Big Bank Hedge Funds

These hedge funds are under the aegis of major investment banks and financial firms. They embrace a wide variety of strategies, but have one thing in common: They were designed (or in many cases, acquired) to keep wealthy clients' money in-house instead of seeing it siphoned off to independent hedge funds.

- AIG Global Investment Group
- Bank of America Capital Markets
- Blackstone Alternative Asset Management
- CSFB Alternative Capital (Credit Suisse)
- DB Absolute Return Strategies
- Goldman Sachs Asset Management
- Harris Alternatives
- J.P. Morgan Alternative Asset Management
- Lehman Brothers Alternative Investment Management
- RBS Asset Management
- UBS Global Asset Management

Funds of Hedge Funds

Funds of hedge funds may seem like a simple concept, but there's a lot of work involved in picking the right mix of strategies, risk and returns to create a working fund. These companies assess hedge funds as closely as a mutual fund assesses stocks in order to find winning managers and strategies.

- Arden Asset Management
- EIM Group
- Pacific Alternative Asset Management Co.
- Tremont Capital Management

Top 20 Moneymakers, 2006

1. James Simons, Renaissance Capital . . . .$1.7 billion

2. Kenneth Griffin, Citadel Investment Group . . . .$1.4 billion

3. Edward Lampert, ESL . . . .$1.3 billion

4. George Soros, Soros Fund Management . . . .$950 million

5. Steven Cohen, SAC Capital Advisors . . . .$900 million
6. Bruce Kovner, Caxton Associates . . . .$715 million

7. Paul Tudor Jones II, Tudor Investment Corp. . . . .$690 million

8. Timothy Barakett, Atticus Capital . . . .$675 million

9. David Tepper, Appaloosa Management . . . .$670 million

10. Carl Icahn, Icahn Partners . . . .$600 million

11. John Arnold, Centaurus Advisors . . . .$400 million

12. Israel Englander, Millennium Partners . . . .$400 million

13. Marc Lasry, Avenue Capital Group . . . .$400 million

14. Raymond Dalio, Bridgewater Associates . . . .$350 million

15. T. Boone Pickens, BP Capital Management . . . .$340 million

16. David Slager, Atticus Capital . . . .$340 million

17. Glenn Dubin, Highbridge Capital Management . . . .$300 million

18. Henry Swieca, Highbridge Capital Management . . . . . .$300 million

19. James Pallotta, Tudor Investment Corp. . . . .$300 million

20. Daniel Och, Och-Ziff Capital Management Group . . . .$275 million

For its rankings on compensation, Alpha magazine included the managers' share of the firm's management fees, usually 2 percent, and performance fees (share of the profits) which typically start at 20 percent.

To make Alpha's list, a manager needed to earn at least $240 million last year, nearly double the amount in 2005. That is up from a minimum of $30 million in 2001 and 2002. Combined, the top 25 hedge fund managers last year earned $14 billion.

Source: Alpha magazine. April 2007

Associations/News & Research Links

Hedge Fund Association: http://www.thehfa.org
Click on "About Hedge Funds" or "Hedge Fund Articles" for information about the hedge fund industry.

Managed Funds Association: http://www.mfainfo.org/index.htm
Includes news (press releases and news coverage), legislation and congressional testimony, and related links.

Hedge Fund Marketing Alliance: http://www.hedgefundmarketing.org

Alternative Investment Management Association: http://www.aima.org
Includes bibliography and additional resources.

Dome Capital Management
They publish the Web newsletter, Hedge Fund
(http://www.hedgefundnews.com)

Eureka Hedge Advisors PTE, Ltd.
http://www.eurekahedge.com

Hedgefund.com: http://www.hedgefund.com
Hedge fund research and information for a variety of audiences. Free access to current hedge fund indices, yearly research, and informational articles

Hedge Funds Research
http://www.hfr.com/

Maintains an internal database of 2500 hedge funds (U.S. and International)

Phone: (312) 658-0958.

Hennessee Hedge Fund Advisory Group
http://www.hedgefnd.com/

Maintains a database of over 1,400 managers. Also publishes the WPG-Hennessee Hedge Fund Index available through Bloomberg.

Tremont Advisers, Inc.'s TASS Research
https://www.tassresearch.com/indexS.cfm

The TASS Database covers more than 2,400 hedge funds and their managers.

Charter House, 13-15 Carteret Street, London SW1H 9DJ

Daily News about the Hedge Fund Industry

Hedge World
http://www.hedgeworld.com

Many features are marked "open access," but registration is required for other features.

Hedge Fund Center
http://www.hedgefundcenter.com

Good source of news information; employment database also available.

Hedge Fund News
http://www.hedgefundnews.com

Requires registration (free); site contains news and listings of different funds (for Contact information).

Albourne Village
http://www.albournevillage.com

Hedge Fund Intelligence
http://www.hedgefundintelligence.com Research Links

Baker Library Guide to Hedge Funds
http://www.library.hbs.edu/hedgefunds/index_print.htm Provides definitions, general facts, and additional resources.

BARRA
http://www.barra.com/research/

This site has full-text articles with a search engine.

Hedge Fund Indices

ABN AMRO Eureka hedge Asia Index
http://monthly.eurekahedge.com/

Performance index on the Asian hedge fund marketplace. Free registration required to access this data.

CSFB/Tremont Hedge Fund Index
http://www.hedgeindex.com/index.cfm

Hedge Fund Consistency Index
http://www.hedgefund-index.com/

The Hedge Fund Consistency Index ranks and profiles over 1,600 hedge funds based on this consistency index, which compares total return (in excess of the risk-free rate of return) to the total of all interim maximum draw downs (interim equity declines).

Hennessee Hedge Fund Indices
http://www.hennesseegroup.com

Includes data going back 10 years. The Hennessee Group, a hedge fund consulting firm, generates these data. (They are not money managers.)

Magnum Funds
http://www.magnumfund.com

With free required registration, this web site provides access to newsletters and reports about hedge funds and recent performance in the sector.

MAR (Managed Account Reports, Inc.)
http://www.marhedge.com

Leads users to all kinds of hedge fund rankings and performance information. See "Directories" for information on their print publication.

MSCI Hedge Fund Indices
http://www.msci.com/hedge/index.html SEC Investment Adviser Public Disclosure (IAPD) http://www.adviserinfo.sec.gov This Web site provides access to registration documents filed by more than

9,000 registered investment advisers.

The Hedge Fund Center
http://www.hedgefundcenter.com/index.cfm

The "Basics" section of this site provides some useful background information on hedge funds.

Van Hedge Fund Indices
http://www.hedgefund.com/vanind.htm

Hedge fund performance indices for various markets: The VAN database, which is used in construction of the Index, contains detailed information on approximately 5,000 hedge funds (2,650 U.S. and 2,350 offshore). These funds represent approximately U.S. $200 billion in assets.

Glossary

Absolute return: An absolute return manager is one without a benchmark who is expected to achieve positive returns no matter what market conditions. Hedge fund managers are also referred to as absolute return managers where they are expected to have positive returns even if the markets are declining. This compares with mutual fund managers who have relative return objectives when compared with their benchmarks.

Accredited investors: Rule 501 (d) of the SEC provides a ready definition of an "accredited investor." Generally, for individuals, it is an individual having a net worth in excess of $1,000,000 or income in excess of $200,000 individually or $300,000 jointly with a spouse, in each of the two most recent years with an expectation that these income levels will continue.

Administrator: The offshore fund entity that manages the back office work and individual accounts for the fund.

Alpha: Alpha is the measure of a fund's average performance independent of the market, (i.e. if the market return was zero). For example, if a fund has an alpha of 2.0, and the market return was 0 percent for a given month, then the fund would, on average, return 2 percent for the month.

AML (Anti Money Laundering from the Patriot Act): The Patriot Act was adopted in response to the September 11 terrorist attacks. The Patriot Act is intended to strengthen U.S. measures to prevent, detect, and prosecute international money laundering and the financing of terrorism. These efforts include new anti-money laundering (AML) tools that impact the banking, financial, and investment communities.

Arbitrage: Arbitrage involves the simultaneous purchase and sale of a security or pair of similar securities to profit from a pricing discrepancy. This could be the purchase and sale of the identical item in different markets to make profits - for example there could be an arbitrage opportunity in the price of gold that is sold more expensively in London than in New York. In this case the arbitrageur would buy gold in New York and sell in London, profiting from the price differential. This could be applied to a variety of transactions: foreign exchange, mortgages, futures, stocks, bonds, silver or other commodities in one market for sale in another at a profit.

Asset classes: Asset class means a type of investment, such as stocks, bonds, real estate, or cash.

AUM: Assets under management.

Benchmark: A benchmark is a standard that is used for comparison for performance. The benchmarks normally used by mutual fund managers are the S&P 500 or the Dow Jones industrial average.

Beta: Beta is the measure of a fund's volatility relative to the market. (Almost all fund managers correlate themselves to the S&P 500). A beta of greater than 1.0 indicates that the fund is more volatile than the market; a beta of less than 1.0 indicates that the fund is less volatile than the market. For example, if the market rises 1 percent and a fund has a beta greater than 2.5, the fund will rise, on average, 2.5 percent. For a fund with a beta of 0.4, if the market rises 1 percent, the fund will rise on average, 0.4 percent. The relationship is the same in a falling market. (Note that funds can have a negative beta, meaning that on average they rise when the market falls and vice versa.)

Bottom-up investing: An approach to investing that seeks to identify well-performing individual securities before considering the impact of economic trends.

Capital structure arbitrage: An investment strategy that seeks to exploit pricing inefficiencies in a firm's capital structure. Strategy will entail purchasing the undervalued security, and selling the overvalued, expecting the pricing disparity between the two to close out.

CFA: Chartered financial analyst. An individual who has passed tests in economics, accounting, security analysis, and money management, administered by the Institute of Chartered Financial Analysts of the Association for Investment Management and Research (AIMR). Such an individual is also expected to have at least three years of investment-related experience, and meet certain standards of professional conduct. These individuals have an extensive economic and investing background and are competent at a high level of analysis. Individuals or corporations utilize their services as security analysts, portfolio managers or investment advisors.

Commodity: A physical substance, such as food, grains, or metals, which is interchangeable with another product of the same type, and which investors buy or sell, usually through futures contracts. The price of the commodity is subject to supply and demand.

Convertible arbitrage: An investment strategy that seeks to exploit pricing inefficiencies between a convertible bond and the underlying stock. A manager will typically long the convertible bond and short the underlying stock.

Convertible bond: Convertible bond is a bond that can be exchanged, at the option of the holder, for a specific number of shares of a company's stock (preferred or common). Convertible bonds tend to have lower interest rates than the non-convertibles because they also increase in value as the price of the underlying stock rises. In this way, convertible bonds offer some of the benefits of both stock and bonds since they earn interest like bonds and appreciate in value like stocks.

Corporate debt: Non-government-issued, interest-bearing or discounted debt instrument that obligates the issuing corporation to pay the bondholder a specified sum of money at specific intervals and to repay the principal amount of the loan at maturity. It is a bond issued by a corporation, for example AT&T or Ford.

CPA: A certified public accountant is an individual who has received state certification to practice accounting.

Currencies: Any form of money that is in public circulation. The main traded currencies are the U.S. dollar, Japanese Yen, British pound and the Euro.

Derivative: A financial instrument whose characteristics and value depend upon the characteristics and value of an underlier, typically a commodity, bond, equity or currency. Examples of derivatives include futures and options. Advanced investors sometimes purchase or sell derivatives to manage the risk associated with the underlying security, to protect against fluctuations in value, or to profit from periods of inactivity or decline.

Distressed securities investing: Investment strategy focusing on troubled or restructuring companies at deep discounts through stocks, fixed income, bank debt or trade claims. Seeks to exploit possible pricing inefficiencies caused by the lack of large institutional investor participation.

Diversification: Minimizing of non-systematic portfolio risk by investing assets in several securities and investment categories with low correlation between each other.

Dow Jones Industrial Average: This is a price-weighted average of 30 actively traded blue chip stocks, primarily industrials. The 30 stocks are chosen by the editors of The Wall Street Journal (which is published by Dow Jones & Company), a practice that dates back to the beginning of the century. The Dow is computed using a price-weighted indexing system, rather than the more common market cap-weighted indexing system.

DTC system: "DTC" means depositary trust company. This is a central repository through which members electronically transfer stock and bond certificates (a clearinghouse facility). The depository trust company was set up to provide an infrastructure for settling trades in municipal, mortgage-backed and corporate securities in a cost-efficient and timely manner. The "system" refers to the mechanism whereby trades are matched up at the DTC.

Emerging markets investing: A generally long-only investment strategy which entails investing in geographic regions that have undeveloped capital markets and exhibit high growth rates and high rates of inflation. Investing in emerging markets can be very volatile, and may also involve currency risk, political risk, and liquidity risk.

Endowments: A permanent fund bestowed upon an individual or institution, such as a university, museum, hospital, or foundation, to be used for a specific purpose.

Equity: Ownership interest in a corporation in the form of common stock or preferred stock.

Euroclear: Settlement system for domestic and international securities transactions, covering stocks, bonds and a variety of investment funds. In addition, Euroclear also acts as the central securities depository (CSD) for several European markets. www.Euroclear.com

Event-driven investing: Investment strategy seeking to identify and exploit pricing inefficiencies that have been caused by some sort of corporate event, such as a merger, spin-off, distressed situation, or recapitalization.

Financial instruments: An instrument having monetary value or recording a monetary transaction. Stocks, bonds, options and futures are all examples of financial instruments.

Fixed income: A fixed income security is a bond; a debt investment that provides a return in the form of fixed periodic payments (coupons) and eventual return of principle at maturity. Types of bonds include:

Corporate bond: A bond issued by a corporation, ex: AT&T or Ford

Municipal bond: A bond issued by a municipality. Ex: New York City or Travis County. These bonds are generally tax free, so you pay no taxes on the interest you earn, but the interest rate is usually lower than for a taxable bond.

Treasury bond: A bond issued by the U.S. Government. These are considered safe investments because they are backed by the taxing authority of the U.S. government, and the interest on Treasury bonds is not subject to state income tax. T-bonds have maturities greater than 10 years, while notes and bills have lower maturities.

Treasury note: The only difference between a Treasury note and a Treasury bond is that a Treasury note is issued for a shorter time, usually two to five years.

Treasury bill: This is held for a shorter time than either a Treasury bond or a Treasury note - usually three, six, or nine months to two years. Interest on T-bills is paid at the time the bill matures.

Zero-coupon bonds: A bond that generates no periodic interest payments but is issued at a discount from face value. The return is realized at maturity.

Fixed income arbitrage: Investment strategy that seeks to exploit pricing inefficiencies in fixed income securities and their derivative instruments.

Typical investment will involve making long a fixed income security or related instrument that is perceived to be undervalued, and shorting a similar, related fixed income security or related instrument.

FTSE (London): The Financial Times Stock Exchange 100 stock index, a market cap weighted index of stocks traded on the London Stock Exchange. Similar to the S&P 500 in the United States.

Fund of funds: Investment partnership that invests in a series of other funds. A fund of funds' portfolio will typically diversify across a variety of investment managers, investment strategies, and subcategories.

Fundamental analysis: Analysis of the balance sheet and income statements of companies in order to forecast their future stock price movements.

General ledge entries: A book of final entry summarizing all of a company's financial transactions, through offsetting debit and credit accounts.

General partner: Managing partner of a limited partnership, who is responsible for the operation of the limited partnership. The general partner's liability is unlimited since he is responsible for the debts of the partnership and assumes legal obligations (i.e could be sued).

Global macro investing: Investment strategy that seeks to profit by making leveraged bets on anticipated price movements of global stock markets, interest rates, foreign exchange rates, and physical commodities.

Hedge fund: A private, unregistered investment pool encompassing all types of investment funds, companies and private partnerships that can use a variety of investment techniques such as borrowing money through leverage, selling short, derivatives for directional investing and options.

High water mark: The assurance that a fund only takes fees on profits unique to an individual investment. For example, a $1,000,000 investment is made in year 1 and the fund declines by 50 percent, leaving $500,000 in the fund. In year 2, the fund returns 100 percent, bring the investment value back to $1,000,000. If a fund has a high water mark, it will not take incentive fees on the return in year 2, since the investment has never grown. The fund will only take incentive fees if the investment grows above the initial level of $1,000,000.

Hurdle rate: The return above which a hedge fund manager begins taking incentive fees. For example, if a fund has a hurdle rate of 10 percent, and the fund returns 25 percent for the year, the fund will only take incentive fees on the 15 percent return above the hurdle rate.

Incentive fee: An incentive fee is the fee on new profits earned by the fund for the period. For example, if the initial investment was $1,000,000 and the fund returned 25 percent during the period (creating profits of $250,000) and the fund has an incentive fee of 20 percent, then the fund receives 20 percent of the $250,000 in profits, or $50,000.

Inception date: The inception date is the date that the fund began trading.

Interest rate swap: An interest rate swap is the exchange of interest payments on a specific principal amount. An interest rate swap usually involves just two parties, but occasionally involves more. Often, an interest rate swap involves exchanging a fixed amount per payment period for a payment that is not fixed. (The floating side of the swap would usually be linked to another interest rate, often the LIBOR.)

Investment adviser: The investment adviser is the individual or entity that provides investment advice for a fee. Registered investment advisers must register with the SEC and abide by the rules of the Investment Advisers Act.

Investment manager: An investment manager is the individual who is responsible for the selection and allocation of investment securities.

IPO: An initial public offering is often referred to as an "IPO." This is first sale of stock by a company to the public.

Junk bonds: Corporate bonds with a credit rating of BB or lower. Also known as high-yield bonds, these bonds are usually issued by companies without long track records of sales or earnings or by those with questionable credit standing.

Large cap securities: Equity securities with relatively large market capitalization, usually over $5 billion (shares outstanding times price per share).

Leverage: Leverage measures the amount of assets being funded by each investment dollar. The primary source of leverage is from borrowing from financial institutions. An example in everyday terms is a house mortgage. Leverage is essentially borrowing by hedge funds using their assets in the fund as a pledge of collateral toward the loan. The hedge fund manager then uses the loan to buy more securities. The amount of leverage typically used by the fund is shown as a percentage of the fund. For example, if the fund has

$1,000,000 and is borrowing another $2,000,000, to bring the total dollars invested to $3,000,000, then the leverage used is 200 percent.

Limited partnership: The hedge fund is organized with a general partner, who manages the business and assumes legal debts and obligations, and one or more limited partners, who are liable only to the extent of their investments. Limited partners also enjoy rights to the partnership's cash flow, but are not liable for company obligations.

Lockup: Time period that initial investment cannot be redeemed from the fund.

Management company: A firm that, for a management fee, invests pools of capital, for the purpose of fulfilling a sought-after investment objective.

Management fee: The fees taken by the manager on the entire asset level of the investment. For example, if at the end of the period, the investment is valued at $1,000,000, and the management fee is 1 percent, then the fees would be $10,000.

Markets (stock market): General term for the organized trading of stocks through exchanges and over-the-counter. There are many markets around the world trading equities and options.

Market neutral investing: Investing in financial markets through a strategy that will result in an investment portfolio not correlated to overall market movements and insulated from systematic market risk.

Master-feeder fund: A typical structure for a hedge fund. It involves a master trading vehicle that is domiciled offshore. The master fund has two investors: another offshore fund, and a U.S. (usually Delaware-based) limited partnership. These two funds are the feeder funds. Investors invest in the feeder funds, which in turn invest all the money in the master fund, which is traded by the manager.

Medium cap securities: Equity securities with a middle-level stock market capitalization. Mid-cap stocks will typically have between $1 billion and $5 billion in total market capitalization (shares outstanding times price per share).

Money manager: A portfolio/investment manager, the person ultimately responsible for a securities portfolio.

Mutual fund: A mutual fund is operated by an investment company, which raises money from shareholders and then invests in a group of assets. The mutual fund manager invests in the group of assets in accordance with a stated set of objectives. The mutual funds raise money by selling shares of the fund to the public. (Usually there are very few stipulations on who can invest in the fund.) Mutual fund managers then take the money they receive from the sale of their shares (along with any money made from previous investments) and use it to purchase various investment vehicles, such as stocks, bonds and money market instruments. Shareholders are free to sell their shares at any time.

Multi-strategy: Investment philosophy allocating investment capital to a variety of investment strategies, although the fund is run by one management company.

NASDAQ: The Nasdaq is a computerized system established by the NASD to facilitate trading by providing broker/dealers with current bid and ask price quotes on over-the-counter stocks and some listed stocks. The Nasdaq does not have a physical trading floor that brings together buyers and sellers. Instead, all trading on the Nasdaq exchange is done over a network of computers and telephones.

NAV: Net asset value per share - the market value of a fund share. Equals the closing market value of all securities within a portfolio plus all other assets such as cash, subtracting all liabilities (including fees and expenses), then dividing the result by the total number of shares outstanding.

Nikkei: The Nikkei index is an index of 225 leading stocks traded on the Tokyo Stock Exchange.

NYSE: The New York Stock Exchange is the oldest and largest stock exchange in the U.S., located on Wall Street in New York City. The NYSE is responsible for setting policy, supervising member activities, listing securities, overseeing the transfer of member seats, and evaluating applicants. It traces its origins back to 1792, when a group of brokers met under a tree at the tip of Manhattan and signed an agreement to trade securities. The NYSE still uses a large trading floor to conduct its transactions.

Options: A put option gives the holder the right to sell the underlying stock at a specified price (strike price) on or before a given date (exercise date).

A call option gives the holder the right to buy the underlying stock at specified price (strike price) on or before a given date (exercise date).

The seller of these options is referred to as the writer - many hedge funds will often write options in accordance with their strategies.

Pairs trading: Non-directional relative value investment strategy that seeks to identify two companies with similar characteristics whose equity securities are currently trading at a price relationship that is out of their historical trading range. Investment strategy will entail buying the undervalued security, while short-selling the overvalued security.

Patriot Act: The Patriot Act was adopted in response to the September 11 terrorist attacks. The Patriot Act is intended to strengthen U.S. measures to prevent, detect, and prosecute international money laundering and the financing of terrorism. These efforts include new anti-money laundering (AML) tools that impact the banking, financial, and investment communities.

Pension: A pension provides post-retirement benefits that an employee might receive from some employers. A pension is essentially compensation received by the employee after he/she has retired.

Portfolio turnover: The number of times an average portfolio security is replaced during an accounting period, usually a year.

Prime brokerage: Prime brokers offer hedge fund clients various tools and services such as securities lending, trading platforms, cash management, risk management and settlements for administration of the hedge fund.

Qualified purchasers: Qualified fund purchasers are individuals or families of companies with $5,000,000 in investments or an entity that holds and controls $25,000,000 in investments. In order to qualify for the exemption offered under Section 3(c) (7) of The Investment Company Act of 1940, all investors in such a partnership must be qualified purchasers or knowledgeable employees for the partnership to qualify for the exemption.

Rate of return: The rate of return is the percentage appreciation in market value for an investment security or security portfolio.

Regulation T: According to Regulation T, one may borrow up to 50 percent of the purchase price of securities that can be purchased on margin. Known as initial margin.

Relative value: Non-directional market neutral investment strategy that seeks to exploit pricing discrepancies between a pair of related securities. Strategy will entail buying the undervalued security and short selling the overvalued security.

Risk arbitrage: Relative value investment strategy that seeks to exploit pricing discrepancies in the equity securities of two companies involved in a merger-related transaction. The strategy will entail the purchase of a security of the company being acquired, along with a simultaneous sale in the acquiring company.

S&P500: Standard & Poor's 500 is a basket of 500 stocks that are considered to be widely held. This index provides a broad snapshot of the overall U.S. equity market; in fact, over 70 percent of all U.S. equity is tracked by the S&P 500.

Series 7 & 63: The NASD Series 7 General Securities Representative exam is the main qualification for stockbrokers, and is normally taken in conjunction with the Series 63 Uniform State Law Exam.

SEC: Securities and Exchange Commission. The primary federal regulatory agency for the securities industry, whose responsibility is to promote full disclosure and to protect investors against fraudulent and manipulative practices in the securities markets. The Securities and Exchange Commission enforces, among others, the Securities Act of 1933, the Securities Exchange Act of 1934, the Trust Indenture Act of 1939, the Investment Company Act of 1940 and the Investment Advisers Act. The supervision of dealers is delegated to the self-regulatory bodies of the exchanges. The Securities and Exchange Commission is an independent, quasi-judiciary agency. It has five commissioners, each appointed for a five-year term that is staggered so that one new commissioner is being replaced every year. www.sec.gov

Securities lending: This is a loan of a security from one broker/dealer to another, who must eventually return the same security as repayment. The loan is often collateralized. Securities lending allows a broker-dealer in possession of a particular security to earn enhanced returns on the security through finance charges.

Small cap securities: Securities in which the parent company's total stock market capitalization is less than $1 billion.

Soft commodities: Tropical commodities such as coffee, sugar and cocoa. In a broader sense may also include grains, oilseeds, cotton and orange juice. This category usually excludes metals, financial futures and livestock.

Sovereign debt: Fixed income security guaranteed by a foreign government.

Special situations investing: Investment strategy that seeks to profit from pricing discrepancies resulting from corporate "event" transactions, such as mergers and acquisitions, spin-offs, bankruptcies, or recapitalizations. Also known as "event driven."

Short selling: Short selling involves the selling of a security that the seller does not own. Short sellers believe that the stock price will fall (as opposed to buying long, wherein one believes the price will rise) and that they will be able to repurchase the stock at a lower price in the future. Thus, they will profit from selling the stock at a higher price now.

Strategy (trading strategy): A "trading strategy" refers to the investment approach or the techniques used by the hedge fund manager to have positive returns on the investments.

Subscription period: The subscription period is the amount of time that the investor is required to keep the investment in the fund without withdrawal, typically one to two years.

Top-down investing: An approach to investing in which an investor first looks at trends in the general economy, and next selects industries and then companies that should benefit from those trends.

Trading disclosure: Trading disclosure refers to revealing actual trades, portfolio positions, performance and assets under management.

Transparency: Transparency refers to the amount of trading disclosure that hedge fund managers have to give to the SEC and their investors.

About the Authors

Aditi Davare: Aditi currently works for a large hedge fund in NYC. Previously she was a Vice President in the Global Clearing Division at a leading investment bank. She has more than 5 years of investment and hedge fund experience.

Holly Goodrich: Holly Goodrich currently works for a large fund of funds in NYC. Previously she was enrolled in the MBA program at the McCombs School of Business at the University of Texas at Austin and had worked in the hedge fund industry for more than four years. Both authors are members of the 100 Women in Hedge Funds organization.

Both authors are members of the 100 Women in Hedge Funds organization.

Michael Martinez: Michael Martinez is a 10-year veteran of business journalism whose coverage of Wall Street appears in newspapers around the globe. He is a former editor at *Kiplinger's Personal Finance* and author of *Practical Tech for Your Business*. He is also the suthor of the *Vault Career Guide to Private Wealth Management*.

Decrease your T/NJ Ratio
(Time to New Job)

Use the Internet's most targeted
job search tools for finance
professionals.

Vault Finance Job Board

The most comprehensive and convenient job board for finance
professionals. Target your search by area of finance, function,
and experience level, and find the job openings that you want.
No surfing required.

VaultMatch Resume Database

Vault takes match-making to the next level: post your resume
and customize your search by area of finance, experience and
more. We'll match job listings with your interests and criteria
and e-mail them directly to your inbox.

V/\ULT

THE MOST TRUSTED NAME IN CAREER INFORMATION

"Fun reads,
edgy details"

– FORBES MAGAZINE

Vault guides and employer profiles have been published since 1997 and are the premier source of insider information on careers.

Each year, Vault surveys and interviews thousands of employees to give readers the inside scoop on industries and specific employers to help them get the jobs they want.

"To get the un-
varnished scoop,
check out Vault"

– SMARTMONEY MAGAZINE

V/\ULT

WARNER MEMORIAL LIBRARY
EASTERN UNIVERSITY
ST DAVIDS, PA 19087 3696